# Rediscover *Jesus*

A Pilgrim's Guide
to the Land,
the Personalities,
and the Language
of Luke

## Peter Edmonds SJ

MINNEAPOLIS

REDISCOVER JESUS
A Pilgrim's Guide to the Land, the Personalities, and the Language of Luke

Copyright © 2007 Peter Edmonds
Original edition published in English under the title REDISCOVER JESUS by Kevin Mayhew Ltd, Buxhall, England.
This edition copyright © Fortress Press 2019

All rights reserved. Except for brief quotations in critical articles or reviews, no part of this book may be reproduced in any manner without prior written permission from the publisher. Email copyright@augsburgfortress.org or write to Permissions, Fortress Press, PO Box 1209, Minneapolis, MN 55440-1209.

Cover image: Photo by Alexandre Chambon on Unsplash
Cover design: Joe Reinke

Print ISBN: 978-1-5064-5961-5

# Contents

|       | Preface                                                                                                 | 5   |
|-------|---------------------------------------------------------------------------------------------------------|-----|
| I     | **Prologue**<br>– *Meeting Luke*                                                                        | 7   |
| II    | **Most Excellent Theophilus**<br>– *Introductory Topics*                                                | 15  |
| III   | **"Let Us Go Now to Bethlehem"**<br>– *Luke's Infancy Story*                                            | 31  |
| IV    | **All That Jesus Did and Taught from the Beginning**<br>– *Luke's Portrait of Jesus*                    | 43  |
| V     | **"Blessed Are the Eyes That See What You See"**<br>– *Luke's Portrait of a Disciple*                   | 59  |
| VI    | **"What Must I Do to Inherit Eternal Life?"**<br>– *The Response of a Disciple*                         | 79  |
| VII   | **His Exodus, Which He Was to Accomplish in Jerusalem**<br>– *Jesus Prepares the Disciples for His Passion* | 93  |
| VIII  | **"He Has Done Nothing to Deserve Death"**<br>– *Luke's Account of the Passion*                         | 105 |
| IX    | **"Were Not Our Hearts Burning within Us?"**<br>– *Luke's Easter Sunday*                                | 117 |
| X     | **Epilogue**<br>– *Living Out Luke's Vision*                                                            | 129 |

## Appendices

| I  | **Praying with the Gospels: Lectio Divina** | 137 |
|----|---------------------------------------------|-----|
| II | **Questions on Luke**                       | 139 |

# Preface

The invitation came out of the blue. Somebody teaching and living in the Holy Land would normally have given this course. I had been there thirty years before and I thought that would be that. Most of the thirty years that followed were spent teaching the New Testament, first in Zimbabwe and then in Kenya. The invitation was to provide the study component of a month's course entitled, "Rediscover Jesus in the land . . . with Luke," to be offered in Jerusalem. I did not know who would make up the group that was "rediscovering" Jesus.

There were obvious contrasts with any conventional course on Luke. The make-up of the group was random: it contained twenty-nine people, ranging from a retired Benedictine abbot to a former German policeman, a young man still engaged in study. Most were lay people, some holding positions in education offices, parishes, or school leadership. There was a seminarian. There were two former Mother Generals. The majority were Australian, but there were also participants from the Philippines, the USA, Canada, India, Nigeria, Ireland, and England.

The other contrast was the lack of stability. Some days were spent at base, but on others there were strenuous excursions in rugged surroundings and extreme summer heat. In the background were the complexities caused by the coexistence of Judaism, Islam, and Christianity in the same city, to say nothing of the divisions between the Christian groups. There were the shopping opportunities in the bazaars of the Old City. There was the attempt to squeeze the best of the normal three-month course into one month. There would be little time for quiet personal study.

The Lucan material had to be treated in a way that fit in with the itineraries of the group. This turned out to be relatively easy. The days given to acclimatization were devoted to initial contacts with Luke. Hence the first two chapters, entitled "Meeting Luke" and "Introductory Topics." Excursions to Ein

Karem and Bethlehem demanded concentration on Luke's Infancy story, the third chapter.

The five-day expedition to Galilee gave an opportunity to establish Luke's special portrait of Jesus and his particular understanding of the challenge of discipleship, the fourth and fifth chapters. The sixth chapter focuses on a block of material from Luke's journey narrative about various forms a life of discipleship might take.

After Galilee, it was time back in Jerusalem to enter into the suffering of Jesus. The seventh chapter explores how Jesus prepared his disciples for this ordeal and the eighth gives an overview of how Luke tells the story of the death of Jesus. The ninth chapter goes through Luke's version of the Easter story. An epilogue discusses the place of the Bible in the life of every Christian, and concludes with insights and memories that the pilgrims themselves declared remained vivid for them after their month spent with Luke.

But how did it all go? This is how one participant described what we did:

*We learned to focus on what was actually written; to recognize Luke's personality traits and his audience; to keep strictly to the information given; to look for insights the actual Greek words give to the text. A new, disciplined world gradually transformed the whole story.*

The text that follows represents on paper what we covered in our meetings together. It is presented here in the hope that it will help others "to rediscover Jesus," even though they may not be able to do this "in the land." It also offers a more permanent record for the pilgrims who did spend a month "in the land."

Individuals and groups may be helped by the topics suggested for "further reflection and discussion" at the end of each chapter, by the 'questions and answers" offered at the end of the final chapter, and by the material of the two appendices, both of which could equally well have been placed at the beginning of the book rather than at its end.

Peter Edmonds SJ<br>
Campion Hall, Oxford<br>
July 2007

# I. Prologue

## Meeting Luke

In June 2006, on Pentecost Sunday, twenty-nine men and women, religious and laity, came to Jerusalem to "Rediscover Jesus in the land ... with Luke." They were participants in the one-month "Biblical Formation Course" offered by the Sisters of Sion at their Ecce Homo Centre, situated right in the middle of the Old City of Jerusalem. As pilgrims, they were anxious to see the land where the events related in the Gospels took place. They were to call this land "the fifth Gospel." But they were equally keen to base their experiences of the sacred sights on a foundation of the sacred writings that describe them. They chose to concentrate on the Gospel of Luke because this was the Gospel that they would hear Sunday after Sunday in the year to come. So their thirty days of pilgrimage would begin most mornings with up to two hours devoted to Luke. What follows is a summary of the material covered in these daily sessions.

In order to get to know this evangelist Luke, who would accompany us, we did not take the traditional approach of discussing who he was, where he came from, and where he found his material, but we took a passage that occurs toward the end of his book, his version of the arrest of Jesus. We wanted to meet him at work in his workshop, to learn for ourselves his attitudes to his material and to compare and contrast his work with that of other evangelists. We wanted from the first to be immersed in the text of this author who would be our daily companion for the month to come.

### The Arrest of Jesus

One of the intriguing features of the traditions about Jesus recorded in the Gospels is the fact that some occur only in one Gospel (which we call "single tradition"); some occur in two Gospels ("double tradition"); and some in three Gospels ("triple tradition"). A few are found in all four Gospels. We took an example of this last type, the story of the arrest of Jesus. These four versions of the tradition are obviously describing the same event, but each writer reports it in his own way. By examining their similarities and differences, we enter into the world of each evangelist and we can gain some idea of their intention in writing in the way that they do. We learn to appreciate too the richness of the Gospels, as we view the same traditions from more than one point of view. Four photographs of the same person are obviously more valuable than one.

The first stage in an exercise such as this is to attempt to tell the story in our own words without reference to the New Testament. We may have heard the story many times and know enough to tell it for ourselves, but it is most unlikely that our version will be identical to that of any evangelist. If we proceed this way, we will find the actual texts, in the order of Mark, Matthew, Luke, and John, much more fascinating. The translations offered are literal translations from the original Greek.

### The arrest of Jesus as Mark tells it (Mark 14:43–50)

Mark's account falls into two paragraphs. The first concludes the story with the arrest of Jesus. The second adds details that really belong to the first.

> [43] *And immediately, while he was still speaking, Judas comes, one of the Twelve, and with him a crowd with swords and clubs from the chief priests and scribes and the elders.* [44]*Now the one betraying him, had given them a sign, saying, "The one I shall kiss is the man; seize him, and lead him away safely."* [45]*And coming, immediately going up to him, he says, "Rabbi." And he kissed him.* [46]*They laid hands on him and seized him.*
>
> [47] *But one of those who stood by, drawing his sword, struck the slave of the high priest and cut off his ear.* [48]*And answering Jesus said to them, "Have you come out as against a robber,*

> with swords and clubs to capture me? ⁴⁹Day after day, I was with you in the temple teaching and you did not seize me. But let the scriptures be fulfilled." ⁵⁰And abandoning him, they fled, all of them.

We note the passivity of the Jesus whom Mark introduced as the "Christ, the Son of God" (Mark 1:1). He is silent until the final verses. Judas takes the initiative and behaves as the one in charge. He kisses Jesus, a nauseating detail. Jesus' words, when at last they come, underline the paradox of what is happening. They were treating him as a robber! And indeed, the force they used, the swords and the clubs, could have dealt with a dangerous robber. The word "seize," "overpower" occurs twice; this was revolting treatment for one who had "done everything well; he even makes the deaf to hear and the mute to speak" (Mark 7:37). His disciples, who had been called "to be with" Jesus (Mark 3:14), all abandoned him. These events are part of the "mystery" of the kingdom of God (Mark 4:11). A careful reading brings out some incongruity in Mark's order of events. The swordsman draws his sword after the arrest has taken place.

Mark's Gospel has been described as the Gospel for the beginner in Christianity, the catechumen. It could have been written at a time when Christians were enduring severe persecution, such as the Emperor Nero unleashed against Christians in the '60s of the first century. Anyone who joined their number was to remember the words of Jesus, "Those who lose their life for my sake and for the sake of the gospel, will save it" (Mark 8:35). They could identify with this Jesus who was the victim of the "chief priests, scribes, and elders," that is the religious, academic, and political authorities of his day.

Around fifteen years or so later, a revised version of this material was circulated in a document that we know as the Gospel of Matthew. We now read this and we note similarities and differences with Mark's version, which is being retold for a different audience living out their Christian lives in different circumstances.

## The arrest of Jesus as Matthew tells it (Matthew 26:47–56)

We may divide Matthew's description into three paragraphs.

> [47]*And while he was still speaking behold Judas, one of the Twelve came, and with him a great crowd with swords and clubs, from the chief priests and the elders of the people.* [48]*Now the one betraying him, had given them a sign saying, "The man I shall kiss is the man; seize him."* [49]*And immediately coming up to Jesus, he said, "Hail rabbi." And he kissed him.* [50]*Jesus said to him, "Friend, why are you here?" Then coming up they laid hands on Jesus and seized him.*

> [51]*And behold, one of those who were with Jesus, stretching out his hand drew his sword and striking the slave of the high priest, cut off his ear.* [52]*Then Jesus says to him, "Put your sword back into its place; for all who take the sword, will perish by the sword.* [53]*Do you think that I cannot appeal to my Father, and he will at once send me more than twelve legions of angels?* [54]*But how then should the scriptures be fulfilled, that it must be so?"*

> [55]*At that hour, Jesus said to the crowds, "Have you come out as against a robber, with swords and clubs to capture me? Daily I sat in the temple teaching and you did not seize me.* [56]*But all this has taken place, that the scriptures of the prophets might be fulfilled." Then all the disciples, abandoning him, fled.*

Matthew often follows Mark closely in describing events, but differs in reporting the words of Jesus. Here is a good example. Jesus replies to Judas' opening words with a challenging question. In a major addition to Mark, Jesus addresses the one who drew his sword with the three items of teaching that make up the second paragraph. He first reminds this disciple of his teaching in the Sermon on the Mount about making the violent man no resistance (Matthew 5:39). Secondly, his words about his Father recall his earlier explanation of the mutual knowledge of Father and Son (Matthew 11:27). Thirdly, he refers to the fulfillment of Scripture, a theme that Matthew has made explicit from the beginning of his story of Jesus since the words of the angel to Joseph about his conception through the Holy Spirit (Matthew 1:23). In his third paragraph, Matthew rejoins Mark and refers a second time to the fulfillment of Scripture, adding an explicit reference to the prophets.

If Mark was for the beginner in Christianity, then Matthew is for the teacher of Christianity, the catechist. He has incorporated into Mark's account items of doctrine that would help teachers in his church. "He brings out of his treasure what is new and what is old" (Matthew 13:52). When a student questioned the teacher why their Lord Jesus had tolerated the humiliation of such an arrest, the additions included by Matthew to Mark's text would suggest lines for the teacher to develop in reply.

Around the same time that Matthew wrote, in another part of the Mediterranean world, a further version of Mark's material became available, and this we call the Gospel of Luke.

### The arrest of Jesus as Luke tells it (Luke 22:47–53)

We also divide Luke's version into three paragraphs, but they are very different from Matthew's.

> [47]*While he was still speaking, behold a crowd, and the man called Judas, one of the Twelve, was leading them and he drew near to Jesus to kiss him;* [48]*But Jesus said to him, "Judas, would you betray the Son of Man with a kiss?"*

> [49]*Those who were about him, seeing what would follow, said, "Lord, shall we strike with the sword?"* [50]*And one of them struck the slave of the high priest and cut off his right ear.* [51]*Answering Jesus said, "No more of this!" And he touching his ear, healed him.*

> [52]*Jesus said to the chief priests and captains of the temple and elders who had come out against him, "Have you come out as against a robber, with swords and clubs?* [53]*When I was with you day after day in the temple, you did not lay hands on me. But this is your hour and the power of darkness."*

In Luke, Jesus takes the initiative and is active in each of the three paragraphs. He is in charge throughout. He is not the silent, abused Jesus of Mark. First, he speaks to Judas, addressing him by name, as if making a final personal appeal to him to change his course. Secondly, he puts an end to the violent activity of his disciples. "No more of this," he says, and he heals the wound of the man they had assaulted. Here he is continuing the healing activity of his public ministry. Thirdly, he addresses his opponents assembled in person, explaining how the power of darkness was now at large once more. The reader remembers the conclusion of the temptation story: "When the devil had finished every test, he departed from him until an opportune time" (Luke 4:13). As for the disciples, their flight is not mentioned. They had done their best to defend him.

As we move through Luke, we will ask ourselves for what sort of person he was writing his Gospel. At the conclusion of the explanation of the parable of the sower, Jesus states, "As for that in good soil, these are the ones who, when they hear the word, hold it fast in an honest and good heart, and bear fruit with patient endurance" (Luke 8:15). It is a Gospel especially relevant to idealistic people who struggle to lead good lives in a hostile and materialistic world not unlike our own. They knew that a life lived without Christ was an incomplete life. The Christ depicted in the arrest scene is a Christ who relates to three sets of people. He has a message that fits the situation of each. He is the Savior, Christ the Lord whom the angel introduced to the shepherds at the beginning of the Gospel (Luke 2:11).

For the sake of completeness, we also remind ourselves of how John tells the story of Jesus' arrest. This version is dated after the three that we have read. We do not know whether John was familiar with them, but we soon realize that he has his own special understanding of the events that he describes, which enriches our own.

### The arrest of Jesus as John tells it (John 18:1-11)

We again divide the narrative into three paragraphs.

> *¹Having spoken these words, Jesus went forth with his disciples across the Kedron Valley, where there was a garden, which he and his disciples entered. ²Now Judas, the one who betrayed him also knew the place, for Jesus often met there*

*with his disciples. ³So Judas, taking a band of soldiers and some officers from the chief priests and the Pharisees, comes there with lanterns and torches and weapons.*

*⁴Then Jesus, knowing all that was to happen to him, came forward and says to them, "Whom do you seek?" ⁵They answered him, "Jesus of Nazareth." Jesus says to them, "I am (he)." Judas, the one who betrayed him, was standing with them. ⁶When he said to them "I am (he)," they drew back and fell to the ground. ⁷Again he asked them, "Whom do you seek?" And they said, "Jesus of Nazareth." ⁸Jesus answered, "I told you that I am (he); so if you seek me, let these men go." ⁹This was to fulfill the word that he had spoken, "Of those whom you gave me, I lost not one."*

*¹⁰Then Simon Peter, having a sword, drew it and struck the high priest's slave and cut off his right ear. The slave's name was Malchus. ¹¹Jesus said to Peter, "Put your sword back into its sheath; shall I not drink the cup which the Father has given me?"*

John gives more detail about the arrest of Jesus from a historical point of view and, at the same time, adds deeper spiritual meaning to it. From John we learn that there were Roman soldiers involved in the arrest, and we are informed of the name of the servant of the high priest, Malchus. We now know that it was Peter who drew the sword. The fact that those who came into the garden were carrying torches, ironically reminds the reader that Jesus was the light of the world (John 8:12); only those who walk in darkness need torches.

Jesus speaks around seven times. We learn about his identity, his pastoral responsibility, and his mission. Twice he spoke of himself as the "I am," the words that God spoke to Moses at the Burning Bush (Exodus 3:14). As a good pastor, he looked after his disciples and allowed them to go, in words that recall what he told the crowds in Galilee about himself as the one who does not lose any of those entrusted to him (John 6:39). Finally, he described his mission: he was to drink the cup that the Father has given him. He was ready to obey the directives of his Father. Even in these bizarre circumstances, he was being glorified by his Father, as he had prayed in the prayer that concluded his final speech to his disciples at the Supper (John 17:1). The only fitting response is to fall down before him in worship with those who arrested him.

John wrote that his readers should believe that Jesus was the Messiah, the Son of God, and that through believing, they might have life in his name (John 20:31). This passage helps us to understand Jesus' identity, his concern for his own as a good shepherd (John 10:11), and his fidelity to the mission that his Father had given him (John 4:34).

By comparing these four accounts of the arrest of Jesus, we have entered into the atmosphere of the four Gospels. We recognize that this fourfold source for information about Jesus enriches our understanding of him and his disciples. Each evangelist offers something special. Our task is to enter into the spirit of Luke. We have already learned something of his concern for order, for personal relationships and of his special vision of Jesus, who, even in the circumstances of his passion, continues his mission of healing human sinfulness and physical ills.

## For Further Reflection and Discussion

"If I had been present at the arrest of Jesus as one of the disciples of Jesus, which account of his arrest would I prefer?" Give reasons for your choice.

# II. Most Excellent Theophilus
(Luke 1:3)

## *Introductory Topics*

Pilgrims spend much time on the move. Before they set out to pray at a holy place or visit an ancient site, they have to make preparations. They have to find reliable transport and engage a good guide who knows what he is talking about. They must keep to times of departure and set realistic times of arrival. They must take precautions against heat, dehydration, and blisters. They must acquire decent footwear and buy loads of sunblock. If they do not attend to such matters, they may complete some sort of pilgrimage, but the frustration and discomfort that will ensue will erase the physical and spiritual benefit that should be its fruit.

The same is true when we come to travel through a Gospel; we must make preparations. Out of many possibilities, we chose to investigate four items before beginning our reading of Luke's Gospel.

The *first* was the significance of the Feast of Pentecost. There were two reasons for this. Pentecost Sunday was the day when the pilgrims assembled and it is the writings of Luke that put most emphasis on the Holy Spirit. The pilgrims knew that this same Holy Spirit took part in every pilgrimage.

The *second* was the recognition of the place that journeys took in the writings of Luke. Pilgrims make journeys, and again it is the writings of Luke that put most emphasis on journeys. The pilgrims were going to take their places on the journeys that take place in Luke's Gospel and in the Acts of the Apostles.

The *third* item was the preface with which Luke begins his Gospel. In it, he outlines his methods and expectations. Just as the guide told the pilgrims the day before about the sites they were to visit the following day, so Luke tells his readers about the world they are about to enter. It is his declaration of intent.

The *fourth* was a general comparison of the four Gospels. This was to look at a sort of map. We are in gospel country, but not every part of a country is the same. The north of France belongs to the same country as the south, but the landscape and dialect differ. So with the Gospels. We deal with Luke better if we know in what ways his work contrasts with that of Mark, Matthew, and John. We entitled this "Luke among the evangelists."

Finally, we looked at another example of how the four evangelists approach similar material. Earlier, we examined their accounts of the arrest of Jesus. Now in contrast we compare how they each treat the material with which Mark begins his Gospel. Every good photographer will bring out some special angle in the subject pictured. The Gospel writers do the same in dealing with the preliminaries to the ministry of Jesus.

## The Feast of Pentecost Then and Now

The pilgrims who arrived in Jerusalem on Pentecost Day in June 2006 were not the first to do so. Nearly 2000 years before them, another group of pilgrims had been in Jerusalem. Their presence is recorded in Luke's second work, the Acts of the Apostles. These pilgrims were devout Jews from every nation under heaven (Acts 2:5). Those for whom Luke was writing could identify themselves with these pilgrims. Luke wrote with the conviction that his Gospel was for every nation under heaven. He began his account of the birth of Jesus by naming Augustus, the Roman emperor of the time, the most powerful person in that world (Luke 2:1), and again when he came to describe the opening of the ministry of Jesus, he noted the name of the emperor who was by now Tiberius (Luke 3:1). Luke, like Paul in his address to Festus, the Roman governor of Judea, knew that these things did not happen in a corner (Acts 26:26). Luke's is the Gospel for the wide world. Like the preaching of John the Baptist recorded at the start of Luke's Gospel, it was written that all flesh might see the salvation of God (Luke 3:6).

Because the pilgrims came together on the Feast of Pentecost, they took part in a solemn liturgy that was an invitation to them to ponder the significance of this feast, which Luke reported in vivid detail (Acts 2:1-41). Pentecost is the last of the great feasts of the Christian liturgical year, following on after Christmas and Easter. They reflected how in dealing with humanity, God has always gone beyond the expected. His ideas have not been our ideas (Isaiah 55:8). Through Nathan's prophecy to David, recorded in the second book of Samuel (2 Samuel 7), he gave Israel a clue of his future action in promising that the dynasty of David would last forever. The reality far surpassed this: in the incarnation, God became man (John 1:14). On Calvary, where Jesus died, God showed his presence and power in causing darkness over the earth and the tearing of the temple veil (Mark 15:33, 38), but these were minor wonders compared with the resurrection that followed.

Likewise at Pentecost, the people celebrated the giving of the Law to the people of Israel at Sinai in the past. But at this Pentecost, the Holy Spirit transformed the timid disciples who had deserted Jesus in his hour of crisis, into enthusiastic and vigorous heralds of the gospel. A fitting prayer at this Pentecost liturgy was, that as a result of their study of Luke, undertaken in an atmosphere of prayer and openness to the Spirit, the hearts of the modern pilgrims, like those of the two disciples who set out for Emmaus on the first Easter day, might burn within them (Luke 24:32) and that they might share the joy of Jesus' disciples who at the end of the Gospel found themselves in the Jerusalem temple blessing God (Luke 24:53). Paul wrote that the Spirit helps us in our weakness; for we do not know how to pray as we ought, but that very Spirit intercedes with sighs too deep for words (Romans 8:26). This Holy Spirit had descended on Jesus at his baptism (Luke 3:22) and filled all the disciples on Pentecost Day (Acts 2:4). The pilgrims prayed for the gift of the same Holy Spirit in the days ahead of them in the land of the gospel.

## Journeys and Luke

*Leave your land and your kindred, and come to a land that I will show you. (Acts 7:3)*

Pilgrims are people on a journey. Our pilgrims were special because they were determined to journey not only through significant places in the Holy Land but also through the Gospel of Luke. Luke's Gospel is a Gospel about journeys. The Greek word meaning "I journey" (*poreuomai*) is found more frequently in Luke than in any other Gospel. It occurs almost fifty times in the Gospel and nearly forty times in the Acts of the Apostles. The former begins in Jerusalem in the East and the latter ends in Rome away in the West. The whole therefore forms an account of a journey, but many shorter journeys go to make up this overreaching journey of Jesus and his first followers. When Stephen began his long speech in the Acts of the Apostles, it was to recall the instructions given by God to Abraham centuries before to set out on a journey, "Leave your land and your kindred, and come to a land that I will show you" (Acts 7:3). Luke is a writer for people on a journey.

Journeys need maps. We need a map of Luke's Gospel that divides it into manageable portions not only in order to acquaint ourselves with these journeys, but also for the probes that we will make into the Gospel as a whole. We will learn to appreciate the genius of Luke as a writer, both in his depiction of single scenes like the feast of Pentecost and also in his ability to compose a rounded story. We may divide the Gospel into a prologue and three acts. Each of these includes some sort of journey. The Acts of the Apostles is also a book of journeys.

### A MAP OF LUKE'S GOSPEL

| | |
|---|---|
| 1:1-4 | Preface |
| 1:5–2:52 + 3:1–4:13 | Prologue including infancy |
| 4:14–9:50 | Jesus' ministry in Galilee |
| 9:51–19:44 | Jesus' journey to Jerusalem |
| 19:45–24:53 | The final days in Jerusalem |

## The Gospel

### *The Prologue (1:1–4:13)*

Mark's Gospel began with a prologue consisting of thirteen verses (Mark 1:1-13). Luke expands Mark's beginning to almost four chapters, inserting into it his account of the infancy of Jesus. He begins with a brief preface (Luke 1:1-4); his infancy story consists of seven major paragraphs, which we will later compare with pictures on the wall of an art gallery. Here we simply note the journeys implied in these pictures. The narrative begins and ends in Jerusalem. Mary travels from Nazareth to visit Elizabeth (Luke 1:39-45); Mary and Joseph are forced to move from Nazareth to Bethlehem (Luke 2:1-7). The shepherds of Bethlehem had a much shorter journey from their fields to Jesus' birthplace (Luke 2:15-17). The family returned to Nazareth (Luke 2:39). The final journey is to Jerusalem for the feast of Passover when Jesus was twelve years old: the climax of this journey was the first words of Jesus: "I must be in the things of my Father" (Luke 2:41-52). We also hear of angelic journeys. Gabriel who stands before God (1:19) came to Zechariah in Jerusalem (Luke 1:11) and to Mary in Nazareth (Luke 1:26). An unnamed angel of the Lord appeared to the shepherds at the birth of Jesus, and he was joined by a multitude of angels who descended to earth to sing their hymn of praise and then returned to heaven (Luke 2:9-15).

The second part of this prologue of Luke is an expansion of the prologue with which Mark began his Gospel (1:1-13). It concerns the activities of John the Baptist as he moved from the desert to places around the Jordan river, Jesus' baptism in the river, and his temptations in the desert. During his temptations, Jesus is on the move from the Jordan to the desert and to Jerusalem (Luke 4:1-13).

### *Act 1 (4:14–9:50)*

This first act covers the ministry of Jesus in Galilee. There is no single journey, but there is plenty of movement. We meet Jesus in Nazareth (Luke 4:16) and Capernaum (Luke 4:31); he passes from desert (Luke 4:42) to mountain (Luke 6:12), from synagogue (Luke 4:33) to house (Luke 4:38), from land to sea (Luke 5:1-3). The disciples of Jesus stay with him but he also sends them on journeys of their own: there is the mission journey of the Twelve (Luke 9:2) and one that occurs only in Luke, the journey of the seventy or seventy-two (Luke 10:1). This prepares for the journeys of Peter and John, of Philip, and of Paul that will take up so much of the Acts of the Apostles.

### Act 2 (9:51–19:44)

This second act consists of the single journey that Jesus makes when he set his face to go to Jerusalem. For nine chapters we see Jesus on the move, interacting now with individuals and crowds, with disciples and with opponents. He is the prophet who has to go up to Jerusalem, even though on his first sight of it, he weeps over it because it has not accepted the time of its visitation (Luke 19:41-44). The journey is not straightforward. It involves backtracking and overlap. But the evangelist takes care to remind us that Jesus is on his way to Jerusalem (Luke 17:11; 19:28). This journey to Jerusalem is also the journey that Jesus is making back to his Father.

### Act 3 (19:45–24:53)

This third act is set entirely in Jerusalem, but still Jesus continues his journeys. He goes in and out of the temple (Luke 19:45), but at night he would go out and spend the night on the Mount of Olives (Luke 21:37). He hosts his final meal in a large room upstairs in the city (Luke 22:12) and makes the journey from there to the Mount of Olives (Luke 22:39). Then Jesus journeys, because others force him to do so (Luke 22:54). Pilate, the Roman governor, sends him to Herod, the local dignitary (Luke 23:7). Finally he is led away to Calvary, the place of execution (Luke 23:26).

After his resurrection, he resumes his journeys, accompanying two disciples as they walk to Emmaus (Luke 24:15) and he goes to meet his disciples in Jerusalem (Luke 24:36). The Gospel concludes with his taking his disciples as far as Bethany outside the city and then setting out on his final journey, which completes his journey back to his Father in heaven (Luke 24:51).

Most Excellent Theophilus *Introductory Topics*

**The Acts of the Apostles**

The Acts of the Apostles continues the story of the Gospel and develops themes introduced in it. Again we may divide the work into three parts or acts. The first part concentrates on the life of the first followers of Jesus in Jerusalem. In the second part, the church expands its activities in the world outside Jerusalem, and in the third part, Paul makes his way to Rome.

*Act 1 (1:1–5:42)*

These opening chapters of the Acts of the Apostles show the first Christians living their lives together in Jerusalem. The risen Lord commissioned them as his witnesses who were to go not only to Jerusalem, but to Judaea and Samaria and to the ends of the earth (Acts 1:8). The Spirit came down on them at Pentecost (Acts 2:4), Peter made missionary speeches (Acts 2:14; 3:12; 4:8), the apostles suffered persecution from the religious authorities (Acts 4:7; 5:28), the followers of Jesus lived lives of prayer and fellowship (Acts 2:42). But they stayed in Jerusalem, despite the commission they had been given to journey to the ends of the earth.

*Act 2 (6:1–15:35)*

The impetus for the spread of the church from Jerusalem to the world around was provided by the speech of Stephen. His first words reminded them of Abraham, who was told to leave his country and his kindred and go to a land that God would show him (Acts 7:3). Because of the persecution that followed after the martyrdom of Stephen, the church expanded from Jerusalem in missionary journeys. Philip, one of the seven (Acts 6:5), went to Samaria, traveled on the road to Gaza, and found himself in Caesarea (Acts 8:4-40); Peter worked in Lydda, Joppa, and then went to Caesarea, too (Acts 9:32–10:48). Paul, dramatically transformed from persecutor to missionary (Acts 9:1-19), preached in Damascus (Acts 9:20), and was sent out by the church of Antioch to cities in Asia (Acts 13:1–14:28). His activity led to the assembly of the leading personalities of the Christian movement at the so-called Council of Jerusalem (Acts 15:1-35).

*Act 3 (15:36–28:31)*

This final section is dominated by the journeys of Paul, both as missionary and prisoner. He brought the gospel to the cities of the Roman province of Achaia (Greece) (Acts 16:11—21:16). On his return to Jerusalem, Paul was arrested by the Roman authorities (Acts 21:33). Again Paul journeyed, but this time as the prisoner of the Romans. The climax of his travels in Roman custody was his arrival in Rome where he was allowed to teach about the Lord Jesus Christ with all boldness and without hindrance (Acts 27:1–28:14). Thus the risen Lord found his witnesses in action at the ends of the earth (Acts 1:8).

The pilgrims were to make several journeys through Luke's Gospel. The journeys of Jesus reported in this Gospel provide a convenient framework for investigating the topics relevant to the journeys made by the pilgrims through the land of the gospel. But before turning to these topics, we must respect Luke by paying attention to the preface with which he begins his Gospel (Luke 1:1-4). No other evangelist included such a preface. We are to understand it as his *declaration of intent* and it will be helpful to us to pause over it.

## Luke's Declaration of Intent

The text of this preface is short enough to quote in full. In the Greek it is one elaborate and well-balanced sentence; a good translation should respect the skill and clarity of the original author. This preface informs us at once that Luke is a writer and a stylist, and raises expectations that we can expect fine writing in the work that is to come. His Greek is the most elegant in the New Testament.

> [1]*Since many have undertaken to set down an orderly account of the events that have been fulfilled among us,* [2]*just as they were handed on to us by those who from the beginning were eyewitnesses and servants of the word,* [3]*I too decided, after investigating everything carefully from the very first, to write an orderly account for you, most excellent Theophilus,* [4]*so that you may know the truth concerning the things about which you have been instructed. (Luke 1:1-4)*

There are many points worth noting in this brief, yet concentrated text. We pick out four.

First, he identifies the reader as *Theophilus*, a friend of God or one loved by God. We are to read and hear this Gospel in his company; in fact we may call ourselves Theophilus and regard Luke's writing as a personal communication to each one of us. We therefore recognize Luke as a *pastor*, and should be on the lookout for a pastoral purpose in the Gospel that he wrote. Whoever we are, we can identify with the crowds who assembled in Jerusalem on that Pentecost Day. For Luke, each was a Theophilus.

Secondly, we should note Luke's intention to write an *orderly account*. We must not be surprised when we discover that at times he follows a different order from other evangelists. When we notice such changes, we should search out his reasons for differing from them. Luke has warned us here that he would do this. All this contributes to the common description of Luke as a *historian*, though we should not understand this word in the modern sense but in accordance with what was said at Vatican II about the type of truth we find in the Gospels. It is truth for the sake of our salvation.

Thirdly, we are to pause on the final point in this long sentence. It concludes with the Greek word *asphaleia*, a word that means assurance or guarantee. Luke is offering Theophilus a guarantee in the matters in which he has been instructed or catechized. So both the works that follow, the Gospel of Luke and the Acts of the Apostles, are composed to give solid foundations to Christian faith and conduct.

Finally, we should pause over Luke's reference to the *eyewitnesses and ministers of the word* to whom he expresses a debt. The most important of those known to us is Mark whose Gospel is recognized as the first to be written. Luke's is not the only Gospel to be indebted to it. The same is true of Matthew, and even if John did not know Mark, he shared similar traditions. We are to bear these other three writers in mind as we go through this Gospel of Luke. We have already done this in our prologue, in which we compared accounts of the arrest of Jesus. But we need to go further and devote a section to *Luke among the evangelists*.

## Luke Among the Evangelists

All authors have their special interests and particular ways of writing. It is useful to list some that are apparent in the work of the evangelists. We discuss first Mark, Matthew, and John, as preparation for our reading of Luke. Here we develop remarks already made in our investigation of the various accounts of the *arrest of Jesus*.

### The Gospels in general

The four Gospels are the brief books that open the New Testament. They are not its oldest writings; this privilege belongs to Letters of Paul, but they are the ones that have most influence on the lives of Catholics. They are read aloud at every celebration of the Eucharist. They began to appear at least thirty years after the death and resurrection of Jesus, which is dated either AD 28 or 30. The first three are known as synoptic Gospels because they can be looked at together, so similar are they in content and order. These are attributed to Mark, Matthew, and Luke. The fourth Gospel (John) is sufficiently different to be taken in its own right. We can regard the Gospel writers as siblings belonging to the same family. Siblings have much in common, but each has a distinct personality and their parents will never mix them up.

### *Mark*

Mark may be regarded as the older brother among the evangelists. His is the shortest of the Gospels, just sixteen chapters with 661 verses, but paradoxically he often gives the longest accounts of incidents in the life of Jesus. His Jesus speaks of the mystery of the kingdom of God (Mark 4:11). But he himself is the real mystery of the Gospel. The one whose ministry begins with such success, ends it with the cry, "My God, my God, why have you forsaken me?" (Mark 15:34). The story that begins with the confident announcement of good news in the first verse (Mark 1:1) concludes with the fear of the women expressed in the last verse (Mark 16:8). The disciples who responded to their initial call with such generosity (Mark 1:16-20; 3:13-19) turn out to have "ears that do not hear and eyes that do not see" (Mark 8:14-21). Their leader's last word is to deny with an oath that he even knew Jesus (Mark 14:71). But the reader can pray with the father of the epileptic boy, "I believe; help my unbelief" (Mark 9:24); may respond with Bartimaeus, "Rabbuni, let me see again" (Mark 10:51); and confess with the centurion at the foot of the cross, "Truly this man was the Son of God" (Mark 15:39). Full of paradox and mystery, those who know Mark have good reasons for calling it not only the oldest of the Gospels but the best.

## *Matthew*

Matthew's Gospel is a revision of Mark for a Jewish Christian audience. His 1068 verses are divided into twenty-eight chapters. He expands Mark by beginning with stories about the birth of Jesus and he concludes with resurrection narratives. His main contribution is the five discourses, or sermons, which enable us to call it the teaching Gospel, of which the best known is the Sermon on the Mount (chapters 5–7). Over the centuries, this has proven to be the most popular of the Gospels for the church in its doctrine and its liturgy. Its Jesus is a figure of majesty, worshiped and addressed as Lord. The Magi are but the first of many to worship him (Matthew 2:11). The disciples, although they are of little faith (Matthew 8:26), continuously call upon him as their Lord (Matthew 8:25). He is Emmanuel, God with us. This is the title the angel gave him at the start (Matthew 1:23; Isaiah 7:14), and the last words of Jesus in the Gospel confirm it, because he would be with his disciples until the end of the ages (Matthew 28:20). These final verses have the risen Lord commissioning his disciples to make disciples, to baptize, and to teach all that he has commanded them. The Church in every age is to continue speaking out boldly the teaching that astonished the crowds who heard him in his own time (Matthew 7:28).

## *John*

John is the youngest brother in the family. His gospel with its 879 verses divided into twenty-one chapters, differs from the others to a greater extent than they differ from each other. The figure of Jesus is sublime. He is the Word of God come down from heaven (John 1:1-18). He comes to reveal the Father. He wants to share with humanity God's most precious possession, his life (John 10:10). This is a key word in the first part of the Gospel. This God loved the world so much that he gave his Son (John 3:16). The second half of the Gospel reveals this love of God; he loved his own until the end (John 13:1). Yet the world and his own people rejected him. Jesus speaks in greater length and at greater depth than elsewhere. He has long encounters with individuals with whom the reader can identify. And this is a Gospel full of symbols. We all need water and bread, light and life. Jesus gives true water (John 4:14) and real bread (John 6:51); he is the light of the world (John 8:12) and its life (John 11:25). He demands faith: "Do you believe this?" he asks Martha (John 11:26). At the end of this Gospel, Thomas replies, "My Lord and my God" (John 20:28). This evangelist tells us why he wrote; it was that "you may believe" (John 20:31). When reading John, scholars have suggested that we keep the words *sign* and *glory* close at hand. The first twelve chapters of the book are often called the Book of Signs and the final nine chapters the Book of Glory, but these two themes spill over from both parts of the Gospel. A traditional one-word description of John is to call it the spiritual Gospel. When we speak of the Gospels, we call Mark, Matthew, and Luke synoptic Gospels, because they can be seen together. John's work must be allowed to stand alone.

And we add a similar paragraph on Luke, which should sum up what we have learned already and prepare us for what is to come.

## *Luke*

Luke revised Mark for a Gentile rather than a Jewish Christian audience. His is a Gospel of salvation for all flesh (Luke 3:6). His 1149 verses divide into twenty-four chapters and they begin with a preface (Luke 1:1-4). In this, he makes a special claim for "order." This is reflected by his solemn introduction of Jesus preaching in the synagogue of Nazareth and announcing his mission of good news for the poor. His Jesus is one who is constantly at prayer (Luke 3:21) and who gives an example of perseverance (Luke 9:51). Jesus is constantly on the move and encountering people, most of them in need and lacking status in society. The Jesus of Luke is a Savior for the whole of humanity. He is a visitor to our world, who has come to direct our feet into the way of peace (Luke 1:79). His disciples recognize their weakness. They ask Jesus to teach them to pray (Luke 11:1) and to increase their faith (Luke 17:5). Jesus reassures them in their weakness (Luke 5:1-11), prays for them before he goes to his suffering (Luke 22:31-32), and sets out in pursuit of them when they are lost and bewildered (Luke 24:13-35). If those outside the boundaries of Christianity know anything about the gospel story, it is usually Lucan material that they know. The stories of the good Samaritan (Luke 10:29-37) and the penitent thief (Luke 23:39-43) belong to the culture of the world.

## Preliminaries to the Story of the Ministry of Jesus

But it is time to move from general comment about the Gospels in order to return to the actual text of Luke. We have already considered how each evangelist reported the tradition of the arrest of Jesus. We now examine the various ways in which the evangelists prepare the reader for their accounts of the ministry of Jesus. First we should ask ourselves how we would begin the story of the life of Jesus. We now supplement this by a consideration of what each evangelist wrote. Then we will better appreciate how Luke wanted Theophilus to understand the life and significance of Jesus.

### How Mark prepares us for the ministry of Jesus (Mark 1:1-13)

In his opening verses, Mark employs his most economic style. Each of the topics that he collects is essential for a right understanding of the work of Jesus. His first verse can be regarded as a title for his whole Gospel: "the beginning of the Gospel of Jesus Christ, the Son of God" (Mark 1:1). He begins with the same words as the Greek version of the Book of Genesis. His next two verses are a quotation from three Old Testament books: Exodus, Isaiah, and Malachi, which originally applied to the Exodus, the exile, and the return from exile: he is telling the reader that the story of Jesus is a sequel to these turning points in the history of God's people (Mark 1:2-3). Then he tells of the ministry of John the Baptist, describing his dress, diet, and activity in terms that recall Elijah and the prophets of Israel (Mark 1:4-8).

Then Jesus from Nazareth in Galilee comes on the scene. He is baptized by John and hears the voice from heaven, proclaiming his identity as God's Son (Mark 1:9-11). But before he begins his own ministry he has to go into the desert and be tested, Job-like, by Satan (Mark 1:12-13). The reader now has enough information to grasp the background that gives meaning to Jesus' first words in the Gospel and the events that follow them, "The time is fulfilled and the kingdom of God is close at hand; repent and believe in the gospel" (Mark 1:14-15).

## How Matthew prepares us for the ministry of Jesus (Matthew 1:1–4:11)

Matthew includes all this material of Mark, expanding it and modifying it for an audience that found itself in circumstances that were different from Mark's. His heading describes Jesus as son of David and son of Abraham (Matthew 1:1). He includes a sample of the preaching of John the Baptist (Matthew 3:7-12), adds a dialogue between Jesus and the Baptist explaining why an inferior should be baptizing one greater (Matthew 3:14-15), and expands Mark's two-verse account of the temptations of Jesus into an elaborate threefold story (Matthew 4:1-11). But more importantly, he adds two chapters of infancy material. There is a genealogy of Jesus (Matthew 1:2-17), the annunciation to Joseph about the coming birth of Jesus (Matthew 1:18-25), the story of the Magi (Matthew 2:1-12), and accounts of Herod's plot against the newborn Jesus, the flight to Egypt, and the eventual move of Jesus to Nazareth (Matthew 2:13-23). This whole insertion of Matthew into Mark's material fits into four paragraphs. Matthew adds quotations from the Hebrew Scriptures, which he claims were fulfilled by the events he narrates. Isaiah (7:14 [Matthew 1:23]), Micah

(5:2 [Matthew 2:6]), (Hosea (11:1) [Matthew 2:15]) and Jeremiah (31:15 [Matthew 2:18]) were all preparing for the birth of Jesus.

## How John prepares us for the ministry of Jesus (John 1:1-18)

John's approach is different again. He introduces John the Baptist after five verses and has references to him at different points in his early chapters, but his only function is to witness to Jesus. His final words sum up his role: "he must increase, I must decrease" (John 3:30). He gives no formal title to his Gospel. He describes Jesus as the Word who is now in the bosom of the Father (1:1,18). In the intervening verses, he describes his pre-existence and his career in the world as the word become flesh. He has no traditions to report about his conception, birth, and early life.

## How Luke prepares us for the ministry of Jesus (Luke 3:1–4:13)

Turning to Luke, we should ask how we would expect Luke to write in light of the program announced in his preface (1:1-4). We would suppose that he would respect the traditions handed on by his predecessors and provide an orderly account to help us establish our Christian commitment on firm foundations.

In contrast to Mark, he devotes two long chapters to the story of the infancy of Jesus and of John the Baptist. We will examine these in our next chapter. The material that follows lists first the powerful figures of the time (Luke 3:1-2). He cleverly expands and modifies Mark's Scripture quotation, which introduces it, and he adds the phrase, "All flesh shall see the salvation of our God," which points to the universal mission of Jesus (Luke 3:6). In common with Mark, he tells us about the ministry of John the Baptist. Like Matthew, he gives details about the preaching of the Baptist, adding a social dimension and relevance to it by relating his replies to the people, to soldiers and tax collectors who asked him what they should do. He has him locked up in prison before Jesus comes on the scene (Luke 3:7-20).

He writes in his own way of the baptism of Jesus and his temptation. He informs us that Jesus was at prayer when he was baptized (Luke 3:21). Apart from changes in order, his account of Jesus' temptations is very similar to Matthew's, a fact that causes many to think that they may have shared a common source, which the experts call Q. This alleged source is a hypothesis to account for material that is shared by Matthew and Luke. Either one knew the other or they were dependent on a collection of material to which both had access.

## For further reflection and discussion

Theophilus means friend of God or beloved of God. From the material considered so far, what would be special in his reports about Jesus to his own friends and loved ones?

# III. "Let Us Go Now to Bethlehem" (Luke 2:15)

## Luke's Infancy Story

During the early days of their pilgrimage, the pilgrims spent time exploring Jerusalem and its surroundings. These surroundings included the towns of Ein Karem and Bethlehem. They also had an excursion to Masada, Herod's fortress on the Dead Sea, and spent a night in the Judaean desert. All these places are relevant to the opening chapters of Luke's Gospel and to the people who populate these chapters. His Gospel began in Jerusalem, with the annunciation by the angel Gabriel to the priest Zechariah in the temple. Ein Karem, although it is not mentioned in the Gospel, has long been venerated as the birthplace of John the Baptist and the home of Elizabeth, his mother, and hence the scene of the visitation of Mary to Elizabeth. Bethlehem was not only the city of David, the greatest of the kings of Israel, but also the birthplace of Jesus, and it was from fields nearby that Luke has the shepherds make their way to visit the newborn child. As for the desert, this was the place where John the Baptist spent his time "until the day he appeared publicly to Israel" (Luke 1:80). It was in a fortress of Herod that he met his death.

### Luke's Seven Panels and Four Canticles

It is worth pausing first to enjoy an overview of the material of the first two chapters of Luke, distinguishing the seven major stages of his story and the four canticles that punctuate them.

Luke devotes two long chapters to events before and after the births of John the Baptist and Jesus. He gives this material not for its own sake only but because of its relevance for the understanding of what he will later have to tell the reader about the ministry of Jesus. These chapters are not some appendix added to the Gospel when the rest had been completed, but a necessary introduction to the reader, giving information about God, about Jesus, and about the various characters who have a part to play. They are introduced by the words addressed to Theophilus in the Preface, which we have already considered. They are to give "assurance concerning the things about which we have been instructed" (Luke 1:4).

1. Annunciation to Zechariah
2. Annunciation to Mary
3. Visitation—
   *Mary's Canticle*
4. Birth of John the Baptist—
   *Zechariah's Canticle*
5. Birth of Jesus—
   *Angelic Canticle*
6. Presentation in Temple—
   *Simeon's Canticle*
7. Finding in Temple

**The seven panels**

Luke divides his material into what we may call seven panels and four canticles. We are to imagine ourselves walking around an art exhibition, but we rest our eyes from time to time in order to listen to words of poetry, which we might even set to music. We are to master for ourselves the contents of the various panels and accustom ourselves to interpreting them in terms of each other, recognizing balance and contrast where these exist. Because we have been brought up on a Christmas story influenced by two Gospels, Matthew as well as Luke, and by a piety nourished also by the familiar Christmas crib, we want to allow ourselves, by listening to Luke's voice alone and through entering his world, to become sensitive to what he wants to tell us in his narrative of the origins of Jesus.

The seven panels are easy to distinguish and to contrast. They begin with two angelic annunciation stories, one to Zechariah, the priest, in the Jerusalem temple and the other to Mary, a young woman from Nazareth. These are followed by a meeting of the two mothers, Elizabeth, the mother of

John, and Mary, the mother of Jesus. Mary then proclaims her *Magnificat* canticle. Then we witness the birth of John the Baptist; the climax of this story is the *Benedictus* canticle proclaimed by Zechariah. The birth of Jesus follows next, with a brief canticle sung by a chorus of angels come down from heaven, the *Gloria*. Two panels about Jesus follow. In the first, he is presented as an infant in the temple and welcomed by Simeon and Anna, two elderly and pious people who frequent the temple. Simeon provides us with the fourth of the canticles, the *Nunc Dimittis*. The final panel gives us a story about Jesus when he was twelve years old. He is again in the temple and he speaks his first words. With all this material in mind and at hand, the reader is now ready to hear how the public ministry of Jesus began and proceeded.

**The four canticles**

These are easily isolated, as they are in our liturgical use. In monastic tradition, the *Benedictus* is used in Morning Prayer, the *Magnificat* at Evening Prayer, the *Gloria* at Sunday Eucharist, and the *Nunc Dimittis* at Night Prayer. As prayers, they become more meaningful as we remember the persons who first sang them and their place in their stories. We impoverish them if we simply regard them as interruptions to the , which can easily be omitted. They are like four pillars supporting the rest of the narrative.

- The *Magnificat* follows after the stories of the Annunciation of Gabriel to Mary and her subsequent visit to Elizabeth, and explains the relevance of these events.
- The *Benedictus* is the third part, and climax, of the story of John the Baptist. His birth was announced, he was born, and now Zechariah tells of his significance.
- The *Gloria* is situated right in the center of the story of the angels and the shepherds at the birth of Jesus, and again points to its meaning.
- The *Nunc Dimittis* marks the midpoint of the story of Simeon at the Presentation, and provides a convenient summary not only of this event, but of the whole infancy story.

Each canticle invites us to consider the past, present, and future of the story that Luke has to tell in his Gospel and in the Acts of the Apostles. They make us look back at God's activity in history, at God's initiatives in the events of the birth of the Son, and at what is to come in the life of Jesus and of the Church. In the canticles, the evangelist uses the character to address the reader/hearer directly, to add to that "assurance" which he had promised Theophilus (Luke 1:1-4).

We now look at the seven panels in greater detail:

## Two Annunciations

### The annunciation to Zechariah—The first panel (Luke 1:5-25)

Luke opens his account with a lengthy dramatic episode, which reads like a story from the Old Testament. We are with a priest in the temple at prayer. We remember the story of Elkanah and Hannah in 1 Samuel (1:1-28). The appearance of the angel Gabriel takes us back to the book of Daniel (Daniel 8:16). God is once again taking a direct part in human affairs.

The Old Testament has shown that it was not beyond the power of God to give a child to aged parents. He had done this for Elkanah, as he had done it for Abraham and Sarah (Genesis 17:16). He promised Zechariah that his wife Elizabeth also would have a child despite her years. Because Zechariah doubted this, he was struck dumb. He should have known better. But Elizabeth conceived her child and expressed her gratitude for the Lord's mercy. And there the story could have ended. The story of John the Baptist is now interrupted by the introduction of the story of Jesus.

### The annunciation to Mary—The second panel (Luke 1:26-38)

Gabriel was now sent by God a second time, to Nazareth, a place otherwise unknown, to a person of no worldly status, to a virgin. The angel speaks twice about the son that will be hers. He first describes him in terms of the expectation of her people for a messiah of the line of David; her son would be born through the power of the Most High. He then explains how the Holy Spirit would overshadow her, so that he would have no human father. He would be called Son of God. In this birth, God would be doing something that went far beyond what he had done for Abraham and Sarah long ago. Nothing was impossible with God.

The behavior and response of Mary to this astounding message give an example of Christian discipleship. She was perplexed and she pondered. Even though she did not understand, she offered herself as the "handmaid of the Lord." She was, in words that Jesus would speak later, "the one who heard the word of God and put it into practice" (Luke 8:21).

Artists in ancient times used to paint pictures on contrasting panels, which we call diptychs. They were meant to be looked at side by side. The two annunciations, with which Luke begins his Gospel, are such a diptych. The more we are familiar with the one, the better we will know the other. And now the artistic Luke brings together the two pictures we have already viewed by informing us how the two mothers, and their unborn children, meet.

## Visitation and Canticle

### The visitation—The third panel (Luke 1:39–56)

Luke's third panel helps us appreciate better the two that have gone before. Three things happen. By leaping in the womb of his mother, John the Baptist begins his mission of forerunner to Jesus. Elizabeth is filled with the Holy Spirit that inspired the prophets and she greets Mary as "mother of her lord." She speaks of her in terms that glorified prominent women of the past and form the first part of our familiar "Hail Mary" prayer. (In Judges 5:24, we read how Jael was "blessed among women" and the same was said of Judith in the book of Judith [13:18]). Finally, Mary herself prays her *Magnificat*, adapting the prayer of Hannah, the mother of Samuel (1 Samuel 2:1-10), and anticipating the prophetic canticle that Zechariah will proclaim after the birth of his son, John.

### The Magnificat—The first canticle (Luke 1:46-55)

*And **Mary** said, "My soul magnifies the Lord, and my spirit rejoices in God my Savior, for he has looked with favor on the lowliness of his servant."*

This is the "song of praise" of Mary the handmaid, or rather "slave," of the Lord, as she reflected on the annunciation made to her by Gabriel and her visit to Elizabeth. She had said, "Behold the handmaid of the Lord" (Luke 1:38). Now she gives her reasons for accepting such a role. In its structure, this *Magnificat* follows the pattern of a psalm of praise. She speaks first of her own experience and then about God. God has looked on her lowliness, and raised her up. It was not Augustus, the Emperor in Rome, through whom God had chosen to work (Luke 2:1) or even Zechariah, the priest in Jerusalem, when the Son of the Most High was to be born. Here is the first hint of "reversal of expectations," which is a major theme of the Gospel as a whole.

She tells us in the second part of the canticle how she understood God and why she "magnified" him. Much of her language comes from the canticle of Hannah (1 Samuel 2:1-10) and from elsewhere in the Old Testament.

*His name is holy, his mercy from generation to generation.*
*He has scattered the proud of heart, raised the lowly.*

He is a God of reversal, as will be made clear in the teaching of Jesus, through his Beatitudes, which did not pronounce the rich blessed but the poor (Luke 6:20), and his parables, in which the poor man Lazarus rather than the rich man found himself in Abraham's bosom (Luke 16:23). This was no mere social message of promoting the poor. It would climax in the raising of his Son from death, a fundamental of Christian preaching as in Paul's letter to the Philippians (Philippians 2:6-11) and the sermons of Peter and others in the Acts (Acts 2:31). Anticipating Zechariah in the *Benedictus*, she refers to God's promises to the fathers, to Abraham and his seed forever.

For centuries this *Magnificat* has been part of the evening prayer of the Church. It is one reason why Luke's Gospel is often called the "Gospel of Prayer." The prayer is not the prayer of Mary only, as she showed her gratitude for what she experienced when the angel came to her, but it can be used by any Christian in gratitude for the salvific events of the whole gospel story and for all the benefits that God gives with the gift of life and redemption.

## Two Births and Two Canticles

### The birth of John the Baptist—The fourth panel (Luke 1:57-80)

We now resume the birth story of John the Baptist. Again three things happen. There is the birth of Elizabeth's son and the rejoicing that it brings. There is the circumcision and naming of the child as John, with his parents insisting on this name that means "God has given grace." Then, like Elizabeth before him, Zechariah is filled with the Holy Spirit and he prophesies. His canticle, the *Benedictus,* is the longest of the four and forms a climax to the birth story of the Baptist.

### The Benedictus—The second canticle (Luke 1:68–79)

*Zechariah* was filled with the Holy Spirit and he prophesied saying: "Blessed be the Lord God of Israel, for he has visited his people and redeemed them."

This is the "song of praise" of Zechariah, a priest of the Jerusalem temple. It concludes the story of the angelic annunciation to Zechariah and birth of John the Baptist. Like the *Magnificat,* the canticle falls into two major parts, but this time in the order of God first and human experience second. Zechariah begins by blessing God and giving reasons for doing so. In general, he has visited and redeemed his people. The crowd at the raising of the son of the widow of Nain would also celebrate this visitation (7:16). The disciples on the Emmaus road were looking for such a redemption (24:21). The whole gospel story can be understood as an account of God's visitation to his people. In particular, he has raised a horn of salvation in the house of David, his servant, a theme stressed in the speeches in Acts (e.g. Acts 13:34), as he spoke through the prophets (Luke 24:44; Acts 3:24), through his mercy to our fathers and Abraham (Acts 13:26) and his holy covenant (Luke 22:20). Therefore, he grants us to serve him in holiness and righteousness all the days of our life. There is a direct line between ourselves and the Abraham of long ago.

The conclusion of the canticle is an answer to the question of the people at the naming of John, "What will this child be?" (Luke 1:66). He would be a prophet of the most high, who goes before the Lord to prepare his ways, as Malachi (3:1) foretold. This means that he will give knowledge of salvation and prepare for the one who will bring about the forgiveness of sins (Acts 2:38). He would be an agent of God's tender mercy, so that the dawn from on high might appear to those in darkness and the shadow of death (Luke 3:1-18). This was all in order to direct our feet into the way of peace. Zechariah's words may well refer immediately to the coming of God to his people, but the evangelist can also be understood as referring to Jesus in his ministry.

The language of the *Benedictus*, like that of the *Magnificat*, is derived chiefly from the Old Testament, but it gives a remarkable summary of Christian belief and longings. It comes as no surprise that it has been part of the Morning Prayer of the church from long ago. A devout Christian of any age wants to live out its program every day.

The first chapter concludes all that Luke wants us to know about John the Baptist before we meet him again before Jesus begins his ministry (Luke 3:2).

### The birth of Jesus—The fifth panel (Luke 2:1-21)

The story of John the Baptist began with Herod, the local ruler (Luke 1:5). Jesus' story begins with the Roman Emperor Augustus, and his representative in Syria, Quirinius. Augustus boasted about the peace he had established in his world; the angels will sing about the peace that the Christ child is to bring (2:14).

Zechariah in his canticle had spoken about God visiting his people (1:68). But because there was no room in the inn, Mary and Joseph could only offer the hospitality of a manger, a lodging place for animals, for their child. Those who glorified and praised God when they saw the child were not local dignitaries, but shepherds looking after sheep. But they were the audience for another angelic message, which proclaimed that this child Jesus was "savior, Christ and Lord." Here is the equivalent in Luke of the titles given by Mark, for whom Jesus was "Christ, Son of God" (Mark 1:1), and Matthew, who introduced him as "Christ, Son of David, Son of Abraham" (Matthew 1:1). As for Mary, she continued her role of a model disciple. As handmaid of the Lord, she pondered in her heart the significance of it all. We are not told that she understood.

### The Gloria—The third canticle (Luke 2:14)

*There was with the angel a multitude of the heavenly host, praising God and saying, "Glory to God in the highest heaven, and on earth peace among those whom he favors."*

Brief though this canticle is, it is nonetheless the center of the paragraph in which it occurs. The paragraph begins with the words, "shepherds living in the fields" (Luke 2:8) and it concludes, "The shepherds returned" (Luke 2:20). This central position ensures that the canticle may be taken as the climax of the story in which it occurs.

At the birth of Jesus, heaven comes down to earth. "A multitude of the heavenly host" sing of glory, a glory that Isaiah had heard of centuries before (Isaiah 6:3), and of peace, which signifies "wholeness of person and unity with others," and "good favor." Zechariah had concluded his canticle with prayer for our feet to be directed in the ways of peace. The song of the angels anticipates the peace that the mission of Jesus will bring. "Go in peace," he told the woman who is cured. "Peace to this house," the seventy are to say on their mission (10:5). "Peace," says Jesus to the disciples on Easter day (24:36). When Jesus entered Jerusalem, his disciples echoed this angelic hymn in their praise of Jesus (Luke 19:38). The fullest New Testament parallel to this canticle is John's vision of heaven in Revelation 4–5, in which he views the heavenly liturgy. This canticle is recalled every time the *Gloria* is used in our Eucharistic liturgy.

## Two Temple Stories and a Canticle

### The presentation in the temple—The sixth panel (Luke 2:22-40)

We come back to the temple, where the story began. Jesus, Mary, and Joseph are there because of their commitment to the Law of Moses. The word *Law* is repeated three times. But the *Holy Spirit* is also at work and inspires Simeon to come into the temple and to recognize the child.

Simeon speaks twice. He first prays to God in the *Nunc Dimittis* canticle. He then addresses Mary. Zechariah had spoken of God's fidelity to his promises of old; Simeon speaks prophetically of what is to happen in the future. He outlines the program of the story that Luke will tell in his two books, a story about the fall and rise of many, both Gentile and Israelite. Mary herself will be a sign of it all. The sword that will pierce through her own soul will strike in Luke's final scene of these chapters, when she and Joseph have to suffer the loss of the child Jesus in Jerusalem. As often in Luke, there is a woman to complement the man. He introduces Anna as an example of devoted piety. Her remarks about the "redemption" of Jerusalem bring us back to the beginning of Zechariah's canticle (1:68).

### The Nunc Dimittis—The fourth canticle (Luke 2:29-32)

> *Simeon ... praised God, saying, "Master, now you are dismissing your servant in peace, according to your word, for my eyes have seen your salvation."*

This final canticle is brief. Like the *Gloria*, it is positioned in the center of the paragraph. This begins with the expression, "Looking for the consolation of Israel" and it concludes with the similar phrase, "Looking for the redemption of Israel." Like the *Magnificat* and the *Benedictus*, it owes much to the Old Testament, especially Isaiah. This short canticle belongs to the Night Prayer of the Church.

The "righteous and devout" Simeon speaks like a watchman at the end of his shift. His words sum up the message of the whole infancy story. Like Mary, he is a "slave of the Lord" and, like her, he responds "according to your word." But his canticle expands the boundaries of the gospel. Not only Israel but "all peoples" are offered the light of God's salvation, as Isaiah had prophesied (Isaiah 42:6; 49:6). The reader who remembers this canticle will not be surprised at Jesus' words in the synagogue at Nazareth speaking of the activities of Elijah and Elisha among foreigners (Luke 4:25-27). He addresses his prayer to God as "Master," foreshadowing the community praying in persecution in Acts (4:24). Paul will use the same language of "light for the Gentiles" when he speaks in Antioch (Acts 13:46).

## The finding of the child Jesus in the temple—the seventh panel (Luke 2:41-52)

This is the only story in our four Gospels about the childhood of Jesus, although the so-called apocryphal Gospels report a few legends. Now twelve years old, Jesus is again in the temple, and people are amazed at his understanding and his answers.

Here we have the first example of the sword piercing the heart of Mary that Simeon spoke of. Here Jesus speaks his first words. He *must* be "in the things of his Father." Translators interpret this as referring to the "house" of his Father or the "business" of his Father. Luke may have both in mind. They balance with his final words after the Resurrection when he told his disciples that the Christ *must* suffer these things and enter into his glory (Luke 24:26). He also tells them about the Spirit that his Father promised (Luke 24:49).

We will hear nothing more about Jesus until he is about thirty years old, ready to begin his ministry (Luke 3:23). Luke sums up all these years ahead by noting how Jesus increased "in wisdom and stature and in divine and human favor." This description goes beyond that given at the end of the account of John the Baptist. He simply "grew and became strong in spirit" (Luke 1:80).

Catholics never hear these two chapters read as a whole in sequence in their liturgy. But they are familiar with important parts of it: the annunciation to Mary, her visit to Elizabeth, the birth story of Jesus and the shepherds, the presentation in the temple, and the finding in the temple. These owe their popularity both to liturgical reading and to their status as the five joyful mysteries of the Rosary. The use of the canticles in the Prayer of the Church also testify to the success and relevance of Luke's composition.

## For further reflection and discussion

Contrast Luke's way of beginning his Gospel with that of Mark, Matthew, and John. List the lasting values that Luke is putting before the readers/hearers by starting his story of Jesus as he does.

# IV. All That Jesus Did and Taught from the Beginning
(Acts 1:1)

## *Luke's Portrait of Jesus*

After their sojourn in and near the places associated with the birth of Jesus, the pilgrims traveled north to Galilee. Their first stop was Nazareth; they then moved to Tabgha on the shores of the Lake of Galilee, with its distant view of the ancient city of Tiberias. This fertile and restful place served as a base for a number of excursions. These included visits to the synagogue at Capernaum, to the mountain of the Beatitudes and, on the final day, to Mount Tabor, the traditional site of the transfiguration of Jesus. There was also a long drive to the north of the country to the ancient Banias and Caesarea Philippi, with views of Lebanon to the west and Syria to the north. There were distant glimpses of the snow on the summit of Mount Hermon, which could have been the Mount of the Transfiguration, and an opportunity to clamber over ruins of Nimrod, a fort dating from Crusader times. All too soon, it was time to return to Jerusalem; this was a matter of a few hours in a modern bus, but it brought the pilgrims across fertile plains, over mountains, and finally through the desert area that separates Jerusalem from the Jordan valley. The last days of the pilgrimage, like the last days of Jesus, were spent in Jerusalem.

This itinerary forms a framework for this chapter and the next. In this chapter, we concentrate on Luke's story of Jesus and on the portrait of Jesus that emerges. We consider first Jesus' ministry in Galilee and then his journey to Jerusalem. The final stop on this journey was Jericho. Once in Jerusalem, Jesus engaged in a ministry of teaching in the temple, which turned out to be a series of confrontations with opponents. In the next chapter, we will repeat this journey, but our topic will

## The Galilaean Ministry (Luke 4:14–9:50)

Luke has plenty to tell us about the places that the pilgrims visited, and we base our picture of Luke's Jesus on what Luke tells us about his activity in Nazareth, in Capernaum, and on the mountains of the Beatitudes and the transfiguration. Through seeing for themselves where Jesus had exercised his ministry of "preaching good news to the poor," the pilgrims prayed for that deeper knowledge of their Lord, which would lead them to a closer following. By getting closer to Jesus, they would see how Jesus himself was the fullest expression of the kingdom that he preached. In his ministry in Galilee, we see in Jesus the kingdom in action, the kingdom in word, and the kingdom in conflict. The *kingdom* is not defined, but its meaning is illustrated by what Jesus says and does.

### Jesus in Nazareth (Luke 4:16-30)

In his preface, Luke had promised the reader an account that was "accurate" and "n order" (Luke 1:1-4). He demonstrates the sort of order that he had in mind in the way that he begins his account of the ministry of Jesus. Whereas Mark begins by reporting how Jesus came into Galilee, proclaiming that, "The time is fulfilled and the kingdom of God is close at hand; repent and believe in the gospel" (Mark 1:14-15), Luke takes us immediately to Nazareth where we find Jesus attending the synagogue on the Sabbath day. By gospel standards, the incident is long and we divide it into its five sections. The passage is of sufficient importance to be quoted in full.

#### Introduction and setting (4:16, 17)

> When he came to Nazareth, where he had been brought up, he went to the synagogue on the Sabbath day, as was his custom. He stood up to read, and the scroll of the prophet Isaiah was given to him. He unrolled the scroll and found the place where it was written:

The visit of Jesus to Nazareth is placed much later in the Galilaean ministry by Matthew and Mark (Matthew 13:54-58; Mark 6:1-6). Luke puts it right at the beginning, as if he is saying to the reader, "If you want to understand the story of the ministry of Jesus, this is where you must begin." In Nazareth, Jesus is in his home town, among his own people. As one of them, he attends the Sabbath service in the synagogue. Jesus' presence in the synagogue reminds us of his respect (and Luke's) for the institutions of his people.

During these services, there were normally two readings: one from the Historical Books of the Old Testament and one from the Prophets. Whether Jesus read the prophetic text appointed for the day, or whether he chose one for himself, is not clear. He would read from a scroll and it would take him time to find the place, as he unrolled it. The writing is vivid and catches the tension of the situation. What is he going to read? We recall how a quotation from Isaiah introduced the work of John the Baptist (Luke 3:4-6); what passage from Scripture will introduce the work of Jesus?

### *Jesus reads from Isaiah (4:18, 19)*

*"The Spirit of the Lord is upon me, because he has anointed me to bring good news to the poor. He has sent me to proclaim release to the captives and recovery of sight to the blind, to let the oppressed go free, to proclaim the year of the Lord's favor."*

Jesus reads from Isaiah 61:1-2. A reference to the original will show that he misses out a reference to "the day of vengeance of our God" and inserts a clause from Isaiah 58:6, "to let the oppressed go free," which suggests in modern language a program for social justice. Luke may have been quoting from memory and got confused; it is more likely that these additions and omissions are intentional. There may well be a relationship between Isaiah 61 and the songs of the Servant found in Isaiah 42:1-4; 49:1-6; 50:4-11; 52:13–53:12, which are applied to Jesus elsewhere in the New Testament (Acts 8:32, 33; 1 Peter 2:22). Later he would tell the disciples, "I am among you as one who serves" (Luke 22:27).

The Spirit of the Lord had overshadowed Mary and had descended on Jesus at the time of his anointing in baptism (Luke 3:21-22). Jesus then is an agent of the Spirit of God, a spirit that has functioned in the Old Testament as an agent of creation (Genesis 1:2), that inspired prophets (Isaiah 61:1), and was an instrument of renewal (Ezekiel 36:26). As one anointed, his mission was one of good news to the poor, another reminiscence of Isaiah, "How beautiful on the mountains are the feet of the messenger ... who brings good news" (Isaiah 52:7). This good news is defined by what follows. In Mark, the first words of Jesus were an announcement of the coming of the "Kingdom of God" (Mark 1:14, 15); Luke's report of Jesus' quotation of Isaiah helps us understand something of what this expression might mean.

Luke refers to the poor many times in his work. In his first Beatitude, Jesus pronounces a blessing for the poor (Luke 6:20). He tells the messengers of John the Baptist to report to him about his preaching to the poor (Luke 7:22). Lazarus, the poor beggar neglected at the gate of the rich, is one of few characters in the parables to be given a name (Luke 16:20). In the Acts, Luke reports that there was no poor person among the Jerusalem believers (Acts 4:34).

The reference to "the acceptable year of the Lord" looks back to the teaching about a jubilee year found in Deuteronomy 15:1–18 and Leviticus 25. This would take place every fifty years and brought with it the cancellation of debts.

### *Jesus' comment and the reaction of the people (4:20-22)*

*And he rolled up the scroll, gave it back to the attendant, and sat down. The eyes of all in the synagogue were fixed on him. Then he began to say to them, "Today this scripture has been fulfilled in your hearing." All spoke well of him and were amazed at the gracious words that came from his mouth. They said, "Is not this Joseph's son?"*

A skillful writer, Luke delays the reaction of the people. He gives the scroll back to the attendant, and "all eyes are fixed on him." Jesus sat down (taking up the official teaching position of the rabbi)—only one sentence of what he then said is given to us: "*Today* this scripture has been fulfilled in your hearing."

*Today* is a favorite word of Luke: the angels said to the shepherds: *"Today* has been born for you a savior who is Christ, the Lord" (2:11). Jesus will say to Zacchaeus, "Today salvation has come to this house" (19:9) and to the penitent thief on the cross, "Today you will be with me in paradise" (23:43). The word is prominent in Psalm 95 (v. 5). The Letter to the Hebrews offers a long meditation on this word of the Psalm. "Exhort one another every day, as long as it is called 'today'" (Hebrews 3:13).

The reaction of the people to his words is not clear: if it was favorable (the word used could mean, they "bore witness for him"), it did not lead to acceptance or action. The words quoted, "Is not this Joseph's son?", suggest that their reaction did not go beyond self-congratulation because one they knew had become such a fine teacher and speaker, but they did not take his teaching seriously. The word could also mean, "they bore witness against him," as if the claims and words he was using were far above the station of one who was "Joseph's son." And possibly they were annoyed because he had failed to speak of the "day of God's vengeance" (Isaiah 61:2). These people wanted to keep him for themselves, for he was Joseph's son. Let him do his miracles here in Nazareth.

### *Jesus speaks a second time (4:23-27)*

> He said to them, "Doubtless you will quote to me this proverb, 'Doctor, cure yourself!' And you will say, 'Do here also in your hometown the things that we have heard you did at Capernaum.'" And he said, "Truly I tell you, no prophet is accepted in the prophet's home town. But the truth is, there were many widows in Israel in the time of Elijah, when the heaven was shut up for three years and six months, and there was a severe famine over all the land; yet Elijah was sent to none of them except to a widow at Zarephath in Sidon. There were also many lepers in Israel in the time of the prophet Elisha, and none of them was cleansed except Naaman the Syrian."

Jesus' next words are puzzling: "No doubt you will say to me this parable, 'Doctor, heal yourself . . . Do here in your hometown the great things we heard you doing in Capernaum'" (which Luke does not report until 4:31). Jesus would have said more than this—Luke picks out what he wants his reader to hold on to. Later in his ministry, his opponents would demand "signs" (Luke 11:16), and on Calvary, his enemies would say, "He saved others, let him save himself" (Luke 23:35).

So Luke wants the reader to recognize the shadow of opposition and the cross even in this first public scene of Jesus. Having read from the prophets, Jesus goes on to speak about the *history* of Israel. He tells two well-known stories about Gentiles in Israel's history. In the first, he recalls how the prophet Elijah healed not a widow of Israel but a Gentile woman of Zarephath in Sidon (1 Kings 17:1, 8-16). In the second, he relates how the prophet Elisha healed not an Israelite leper but Naaman the Syrian, a foreigner (2 Kings 5:1-14). Luke is preparing his readers not only for Jesus' prophetic activity in his ministry but also for the mission "to the ends of the earth," which he will narrate in the Acts of the Apostles (Acts 1:8).

### *Final reaction of the people of Nazareth (4:28-30)*

*When they heard this, all in the synagogue were filled with rage. They got up, drove him out of the town, and led him to the brow of the hill on which their town was built, so that they might hurl him off the cliff. But he passed through the midst of them and went on his way.*

This time there is no ambiguity about the reaction of the people. They were all filled with rage at hearing this and made an attempt on his life. At the end of that life, the Jerusalem authorities would drive him out of their city to die on a cross. This tradition is preserved in the Letter to the Hebrews, which records how Jesus "suffered outside the gate" (Hebrews 13:12).

On that occasion, he indeed died but he also rose from the dead. Now, at Nazareth, "passing through the midst of them, he went on his way." In the remainder of chapter 4 we read of Jesus' successful mission in Capernaum. When he came to leave there of his own free will, "the people sought him and came to him, and would have kept him from leaving them" (4:42). Jesus was rejected by the people of his own town, but accepted and welcomed by the stranger.

*Conclusion*

The whole Nazareth incident then is surely to be read on two levels. Not only is Luke giving us a typical scene from Jesus' public ministry, one that is recorded much more briefly in Mark (6:1-6) and Matthew (13:54-58), he is also giving us a sort of mini-Gospel, since this one incident contains in miniature the whole of his Gospel.

- Jesus describes his mission in terms of the Old Testament prophecy.
- The reaction of the people points forward to Calvary.
- His escape anticipates his resurrection.
- The rejection by his own people and his welcome in Capernaum looks forward to its acceptance by foreigners and Gentiles.

A parallel in Acts is provided by the story of Paul at Antioch in Pisidia (Acts 13:46, 47). There Paul addressed his own people but they rejected him and his message. So Paul went to the Gentiles and as a result, they "were glad and praised the name of the Lord" (Acts 13:48).

### Jesus in Capernaum (Luke 4:31-44)

*He went down to Capernaum, a city in Galilee, and was teaching them on the sabbath. (Luke 4:31)*

It was in towns around the lake, rather than his hometown of Nazareth, that Jesus exercised most of his activity. We focus on Capernaum, where Peter had his house and where a building identified with an ancient synagogue survives in ruins to this day. Mark devotes eighteen verses to describing one day of Jesus' activities there (Mark 1:21-39). Luke covers the same material more efficiently in fourteen verses.

The day begins with Jesus in the synagogue, where he expels a demon from a man and wins the admiration of the people for his teaching with authority (Luke 4:31-37). Jesus then goes into a house and heals the mother-in-law of Simon from a fever (Luke 4:38, 39). Then, as the sun goes down, he has to deal with the crowds who flock to him; he cures their diseases and casts out their demons (4:40, 41). As the new day dawns, Jesus is discovered by the crowds out in a desert place. He has to tell the people who are trying to keep hold of him how he must go off to other cities too, for he was sent for this purpose. He had to "proclaim the good news of the kingdom of God," a saying that echoes the end of the infancy story, that "It was necessary for him to be in the things of his Father" (Luke 2:49). Jesus has journeyed from synagogue to house, from open space to desert. This Jesus is not confined.

Mark and Matthew both describe this "day" in their own way. Mark, as often in narrative, is longer and somewhat breathless in his descriptions (Mark 1:21-39). Matthew gives the shortest account. He omits the exorcism in the synagogue and explains how Jesus' activities of healing and exorcism were a fulfillment of a servant song of Isaiah (Matthew 8:14-17; Isaiah 53:4). One could argue that Luke gives the most literary and satisfying version. This is how Jesus "preached the good news to the poor" and "proclaimed the year of the Lord's favor" (Luke 4:18, 19). In the Acts of the Apostles, Peter and Paul would exercise a similar ministry of healing. Peter cured a lame man at the gate of the temple (Acts 3:7); Paul cured a man who had never walked (Acts 14:10).

### The Mount of Beatitudes (Luke 6:12-49)

*Now during those days he went out to the mountain to pray; and he spent the night in prayer to God. (Luke 6:12)*

According to Matthew, Jesus proclaimed the Beatitudes at the beginning of the sermon that he preached "when he went up the mountain" (Matthew 5:1). In Luke, he preaches these same Beatitudes "on a level place" when he came down the mountain where he had gone to pray (Luke 6:12, 17). These days there is a beautiful sanctuary built on the summit of the mountain traditionally associated with Jesus' sermon and the Beatitudes with which he began it.

Here is the reflection offered to the pilgrims when they assembled there for the Eucharist:

Before Jesus selected and called the disciples whom we know as the Twelve, he spent a whole night in prayer on a mountain. We can easily surmise the subject of his prayer. He prayed to his Father as a Jew, as a member of his own people. Foundational to his identity as a member of the people of Israel, was his consciousness of God as Creator and Redeemer. The Bible begins with an account in the book of Genesis of how he created the world. The climax of the opening books of the Bible is the story of how God as Redeemer delivered his suffering people from Egypt and brought them into the land (Exodus 3:7, 8). He would also reflect how often, in the psalms that he prayed with his people, God was portrayed as the God who cared for the widow and the orphan (Psalm 146:9).

When the day came, after his night in prayer, he appointed twelve of his disciples to be apostles, his own representatives. When they came down the mountain, they found crowds at the foot of the mountain, all longing to hear him and to be cured of their sicknesses. So Jesus began to speak to them and the disciples were there to listen too, because as his representatives they would be expected to pass on his teaching.

The Twelve may well have been astonished at what Jesus had to say, but they would not have been if they had made their own the image of God that Jesus had. Jesus knew that in his proclamation of the kingdom, the God who created and redeemed, the God who looked after the widow and the orphan, was again active. This is what was happening in the ministry of Jesus. The poor, the hungry, the weeping, and the excluded had their champion before them, and so they were truly blessed. He had come to bring the good news to the poor. As one scholar puts it, "Jesus calls the poor and oppressed 'blessed' not because their actual position is such, but because the kingdom that he proclaims and enacts will confront those values and conditions that have made them marginal." They were to be congratulated, because they were the ones for whom God loves to act. When we recognize our own need, then God can and will help us.

## The Mount of the Transfiguration (Luke 9:28-36)

*Now about eight days after these sayings Jesus took with him Peter and John and James and went up on the mountain to pray. (Luke 9:28)*

Matthew, Mark, and Luke all tell us that Jesus was "transfigured" on a 'high mountain" (Mark 9:2; Matthew 17:1). This could have been Mount Hermon, the very high mountain in the north of Israel near the present Syrian border, but Christian tradition has favored the rather more accessible Mount Tabor, where a magnificent pilgrim center with a fine church has been constructed.

Here is the reflection offered to the pilgrims at the Church at the summit of Mount Tabor, based on Luke's version of the event.

*(Moses and Elijah) appeared in glory and were speaking of his exodus, which he was to accomplish at Jerusalem. (Luke 9:31)*

Jesus is again at prayer on a mountain. According to Luke's story of Jesus, he has recently spoken for the first time to his disciples of his coming suffering, death, and resurrection. He will repeat this warning to them after the cure of the epileptic boy, which follows immediately after the transfiguration. Just as he had prepared Peter and the others for the events of his ministry and for their part in it by a miraculous catch of fish, so he makes them ready for the events that will take place in Jerusalem by taking them up a mountain for prayer, and it was there that he was transfigured.

There are several divergences in Luke's account compared with those of Matthew and Mark. Only Luke tells us about the *prayer* of Jesus. We have met him at prayer on a mountain before. He prayed all night before the call of the Twelve and his teaching the Sermon on the Plain. Then, he may well have reflected on the nature and character of his Father, the Creator God, the God who redeemed his suffering people. Now he would reflect on the struggles the disciples were having to overcome their surprise and foreboding, as he spoke to them openly about the destiny that lay ahead of him.

This is confirmed by another detail that only Luke gives us, that the subject of the conversation of Jesus with Moses and Elijah was the *"exodus"* that he was to accomplish in Jerusalem. *Exodus* is one of those special biblical words. Its primary meaning refers to the *exodus* of the people of Israel from Egyptian oppression. Similar language was used by the prophet Isaiah to describe the return of the exiled people of Israel from Babylon centuries later. The word *exodus* is now being used to describe what would happen to Jesus in Jerusalem and the effects that this *exodus* would bring about in terms of redemption of people from the forces of sin.

Luke enriches the traditional account of the transfiguration by these references to the *prayer* of Jesus and to the *exodus*. He conforms to the other accounts by including the report of the voice from heaven speaking once again. The voice repeats what was said at the baptism of Jesus about his identity of Jesus as the Beloved Son. But it adds the instruction, "Listen to him." Here Luke ends his story. He simply says that the disciples found themselves alone with Jesus and they kept silent and told nobody of what had happened.

Here we may put aside the text and the details of the text and, with the disciples, concentrate on the person of Jesus alone. At the birth of Jesus, Mary had pondered in her heart. At the cross, his acquaintances simply stand and watch. We may do the same in the spirit of contemplation. We adore in silence the one who is the subject of our prayer, our devotion, and our commitment. Hopefully, we too, standing on the summit of this Mount Tabor, the traditional site of the transfiguration of Jesus, have had a glimpse of the glory of Jesus, and there is no more to be said.

## The Road to Jerusalem (Luke 9:51–19:44)

*When the days drew near for him to be taken up, he set his face to go to Jerusalem.* (Luke 9:51)

Mark had devoted two chapters to the description of Jesus' journey to Jerusalem (Mark 8:27–10:52). Luke devotes almost ten. The pilgrims who were brought back to Jerusalem from Galilee in a few hours in comfort by modern air-conditioned bus, found this rigorous journeying of Jesus with his disciples through mountains and valleys, deserts and plain, a challenging contrast. It was not easy to repeat the words of the would-be disciple recorded by Luke at this point, "I will follow you wherever you go" (Luke 9:57).

During these chapters, Jesus is never alone physically, but he is without confidantes, apart from his Father. In John, Jesus tells his disciples: "You will leave me alone. Yet I am not alone because the Father is with me" (John 16:32). We hear one side of one conversation with this Father when he prays, "I thank you, Father, Lord of heaven and earth" (Luke 10:21). Besides being a model of prayer, Jesus gives an example of the endurance and perseverance that were so necessary for the readers of Luke who lived in a hostile and uncomprehending world. He exemplifies those whom he describes in his parable, "But as for that in the good soil, these are the ones who when they hear the word, hold it fast in a good and honest heart, and bear fruit with patient endurance" (Luke 8:15). He "set his face to go to Jerusalem" (Luke 9:51) and nothing will shake this resolution.

On this journey, he exercises the role of a prophet. As a prophet, he teaches. This teaching is spread out over these chapters of the journey. This makes a contrast with Matthew, who gives us the teaching of Jesus in blocks, such as the Sermon on the Mount, which we call discourses (Matthew 5–7; 10; 13; 18; 24–25). The teaching is adapted to the particular audience with whom Jesus is relating at a particular time.

He trains his *disciples*, with special lessons about prayer (Luke 11:2) and about faith (Luke 17:5). They are his "little flock," which is not to be afraid (Luke 12:32). We will return to this teaching for disciples in our next chapter.

He responds to the *opponents* who hassle and criticize him. Part of his technique is his use of parables, which express his own understanding of God and his mission. Why, they demand, does he welcome sinners and eat with them? His reply consists of parables about a man who lost a sheep, a woman who lost a coin, and a man who lost two sons (Luke 15:1-32). He makes these parables personal, introducing them with the question, "Which one of you?" Sometimes he uses the severe language typical of the prophets of Israel of old times. Such are the woes he pronounces in the presence of the Pharisees, "Woe to you, Pharisees," he repeats three times (Luke 11:41-44).

He teaches the *crowds*, sometimes with parables such as the story of the rich fool (Luke 12:13-21) and at times more bluntly when he warns them of the cost of discipleship. "None of you can be my disciple if you do not give up all your possessions" (Luke 14:33). With such vivid language, he reinforces the message of the Sermon on the Plain, which taught love for enemies and for the disciple to be like the teacher (Luke 6:20-49).

He continues to show sensitive care for *individuals*, such as the woman who had been crippled for eighteen years (Luke 13:12) and Zacchaeus, to whose house he brought salvation after glimpsing him up a sycamore tree (Luke 19:9). We will have more to say about such individuals in our next chapter.

## The Final Days in Jerusalem (Luke 19:45–24:53)

*Every day he was teaching in the temple. The chief priests, the scribes, and leaders of the people kept looking for a way to kill him. (Luke 19:47)*

Luke now moves into material familiar to us from Mark, in contrast to the previous section about the journey, which owed little to Mark. We can distinguish three major sections. Luke first reports Jesus' activity and teaching in the temple, then his last meal with his disciples, and finally, his arrest, trials, and death, culminating in the Easter story. We concentrate on the first section. The remaining two will be topics of later chapters.

### The temple (Luke 19:45–21:38)

The temple is of special importance for Luke. His Gospel begins and ends in it (Luke 1:8; 24:53). On his arrival in Jerusalem, Jesus immediately entered the temple and he returned there daily in order to teach (Luke 19:45-47). He spent the nights at the mountain called the Mount of Olives (Luke 21:37). It is difficult for us today to grasp the significance of the temple for the people of Jesus' time. Not only was it the place where God was thought to have his dwelling, but its magnificence dwarfed the rest of the city. It occupied more than a third of the land space. It gave employment to a third of the population. To this day, the temple continues to dominate the life of the city of Jerusalem. Visits to the Western Wall, a part of which has survived over the centuries, continue without a break. Excavations in recent years have uncovered massive traces of this ancient building, so that pilgrims can tread where Jesus trod.

Luke describes the so-called "cleansing" of the temple more briefly than the other evangelists (Mark 11:15-19; Matthew 21:12–13). Like them, he reports how Jesus quoted Isaiah and Jeremiah, who had denounced its corruption centuries before (Isaiah 56:7; Jeremiah 7:11). Predictably, the authorities question him about the authority that gave him the right to behave in this way (Luke 20:2). He refused a direct answer, challenging them about John the Baptist and their failure to take him seriously. He then entered into various controversies with the chief priests, scribes, and elders who "tried to trap him in what he said" (20:20). The narrative ends with the incident of the widow who put into the temple treasury all she had to live on. At this point in Mark, Jesus leaves the temple and speaks to his disciples at length about its future destruction and about the end of time. Luke says nothing about Jesus leaving the temple, but has Jesus speaking in greater detail about how Jerusalem would be "surrounded by armies" (Luke 21:20). Meanwhile, Luke notes twice how popular Jesus was with the ordinary people in contrast to their leaders:

*All the people were spellbound by what they heard. (Luke 19:48)*

*All the people would get up early in the morning to listen to him in the temple. (Luke 21:38)*

Christian imagination has rightly been stimulated by the pictures in Luke's infancy story, which are set in the temple. The story of Simeon and Anna meeting the infant Jesus there, and the drama of the finding of the child Jesus in the temple after he had been lost for three days (Luke 2:25-51) will endure as long as Luke's Gospel endures. But Luke, as well as Mark and Matthew, who report similar traditions, surely wants his readers to take very seriously this "temple" material situated near the end of Jesus' life. The parable of Jesus about the tenants of the vineyard who refused to hand over its produce, his reply to a trick question about the duty of paying taxes to Caesar and giving to God what was due to God, his affirmation about the resurrection and the God who is "God of the living," and his own question about Psalm 110 that led to his affirmation of his own Lordship (Luke 20:9–44)—all continue to be relevant to the Theophilus who lives in every age of the church. Such teaching provoked his death.

With the coming of the Festival of Unleavened Bread, Jesus makes plans to eat the Passover meal with his disciples (Luke 22:7). The "exodus that he was about to accomplish at Jerusalem" (Luke 9:31), which he had spoken about with Moses and Elijah on the Mount of Transfiguration, was about to begin.

FOR FURTHER REFLECTION AND DISCUSSION

Name three characteristics of the Jesus portrayed in Luke's Gospel that conform to, or contrast with, characteristics of Jesus with which you are familiar from other sources.

# V. "Blessed Are the Eyes That See What You See"
(Luke 10:23)

## Luke's Portrait of a Disciple

The main interest for our pilgrims, as they traveled through the land of the Gospels, was of course the figure of Jesus. Through the Gospel of Luke, their first aim was to familiarize themselves with what "he did and taught from the beginning until the time when he was taken up" (Acts 1:1-2). Yet any reader of the Gospels knows that Jesus was rarely alone. He was constantly accompanied by disciples, and it is this group, who constitute the most important participants in the story of Jesus, who are the subject of our investigation in our next journey through the text of Luke.

By disciples in the Gospel, one usually understands the inner circle of Jesus, sometimes known as "The Twelve." But in this chapter, we want to broaden this circle to include all those who enjoyed a positive personal relationship with him, however brief this might have been. These owe their place in the Gospel story to something they said or did that illustrates an aspect of Christian living for the reader of the Gospel. We also include under the heading of "disciple" characters from the parables of Jesus whom Jesus obviously introduced as models of Christian discipleship.

This chapter involves some repetition of the previous one, in that we go through the Gospel story again. This is to be welcomed in so far as these are texts to which we can constantly return in the expectation of finding something fresh. New questions provoke new answers. The question this time is about disciples and discipleship. We again travel through the way indicated by our map of Luke. We begin in Galilee, travel the road from Galilee to Jerusalem, and stay with Jesus as he enters his last days in that city.

## The Galilaean Ministry (Luke 4:14–9:50)

The first activity of the pilgrims on their second day in Galilee was to sail on the lake of Galilee in a boat, which was a replica of one dating from the first century that had been discovered buried on the shores of the lake. It was the ideal situation for them to listen to the three Gospel accounts of the storm on the lake. They heard first the account of Mark, in which Jesus rebuked the disciples, saying, "Have you still no faith?" (Mark 4:40). They then listened to Matthew, in which his question was, "Why are you afraid, men of little faith?" (Matthew 8:26). Finally, they heard Luke, who reports the question as, "Where is your faith?" (Luke 8:25). This is a good example of how the different communities remembered Jesus and his pedagogy of his disciples. He was their teacher. They were not easy students. The pilgrims could ponder which question Jesus was asking them as they sailed the same waters. The incident of the storm on the lake happens when the Galilaean ministry is well under way. We must go back to its beginning in order to tell the story of the disciples of Jesus. And we must begin with Mark's version of events, because Luke almost certainly knew it.

### The Twelve in Galilee

Luke inherits three positive stories from Mark about the inner circle of Jesus' disciples. These are the traditions about the call of the four by the lake (Mark 1:16-20), the call of the Twelve on the mountain (Mark 3:13-19), and the mission on which Jesus sent them out, "two by two," giving them "authority over the unclean spirits" (Mark 6:7-13). Luke gives his own version of each of these and any discussion of Luke's understanding of discipleship must begin with his version of "The Call of the Four." He tells the story at double the length in comparison with Mark (Mark 1:16-20) and Matthew (Matthew 4:18-22) and we must examine it in some detail.

*Vocation of the Twelve*

*(1) The call of Peter and Zebedee's sons (5:1-11)*

Luke places this first call story later than Mark, who relates it right at the beginning of the ministry of Jesus, and he greatly expands it. Mark and Matthew describe it in four verses (Mark 1:16-20; Matthew 4:18-22); Luke uses eleven verses. He concentrates on the role of Peter and mentions James and John almost as an afterthought. He omits Andrew completely.

We can distinguish in the story the four stages that marked the call of leaders of God's people in the Old Testament like Moses, Jeremiah, and Isaiah. By narrating the call of Peter and his companions in this way, Luke is not only promoting Peter to a status similar to that of an Isaiah or Jeremiah but he is also inviting those with responsibility in the community in his own day to recognize the pattern of their own call and vocation and to draw conclusions from it. Luke has transformed the brief Marcan account of the call of the first disciples into a "dramatic episode" about discipleship, which functions in the Gospel story as a parallel to the "dramatic episode" about Jesus in Nazareth that was so instructive about the person and mission of Jesus (Luke 4:16-30). We comment on the whole text stage by stage.

*The setting (Luke 5:1-3)*

*It happened that while Jesus was standing beside the lake of Gennesaret, and the crowd was pressing in on him to hear the word of God, he saw two boats there at the shore of the lake; the fishermen had gone out of them and were washing their nets. He got into one of the boats, the one belonging to Simon, and asked him to put out a little way from the shore. Then he sat down and taught the crowds from the boat.*

Luke begins his story in the solemn style of narrative books of the Old Testament, *("It happened that")* which alerts us that something important is about to happen. Jesus is preaching the Word of God, an expression common in Luke but rare in the other Gospels (Luke 8:11). The scene is similar to the setting for Jesus' teaching in parables in Mark (Mark 4:1). The closest parallel is the opening call scene of Mark, where the disciples are also washing their nets (Mark 1:16-20). The report that Jesus "sat down" adds to the solemnity of his teaching. This was the posture of the teacher in Israel.

*An experience of God (Luke 5:4-7)*
> When he had finished speaking, he said to Simon, "Put out into the deep water and let down your nets for a catch." Simon answered, "Master, we have worked all night long but have caught nothing. Yet if you say so, I will let down the nets." When they had done this, they caught so many fish that their nets were beginning to break. So they signaled to their partners in the other boat to come and help them. And they came and filled both boats, so that they began to sink.

The fact that Jesus finished his teaching does not mean that he has completed his task. He must move on to call disciples who would continue his mission. The way this came about involved surprise and even shock. Who was this preacher of the Word of God to give directions to an experienced fisherman about fishing? To his credit, Peter did what he was told to do. And the result was an enormous catch of fish. The story appears in another form in the final chapter of John. There we are told that there were 153 fish caught that day (John 21:11).

*An objection, reassurance, and mission (Luke 5:8-11)*
> But when Simon Peter saw it, he fell down at Jesus' knees, saying, "Go away from me, Lord, for I am a sinful man!" For he and all who were with him were amazed at the catch of fish that they had taken; and so also were James and John, sons of Zebedee, who were partners with Simon. Then Jesus said to Simon, "Do not be afraid; from now on you will be catching people." When they had brought their boats to shore, they left everything and followed him.

The story now takes on a pattern familiar to those who know the stories of the calls of the leaders of God's people in the Old Testament. Accounts of the call of Moses in Exodus (3:7-12), the call of Jeremiah (Jeremiah 1:4-7), and the call of Isaiah (Isaiah 6:1-9) follow a similar structure. Each has an experience of God in some way. For Moses, it was a bush that burned without being consumed, for Isaiah a vision of the holiness of God on his heavenly throne, for Jeremiah the hearing of the voice of God. The result was a feeling of unworthiness and helplessness in the divine presence. But God reassures and encourages those he calls, and outlines the mission that he has in store for them. In the strength of this call and commission, the one called proves capable of living out their vocation with courage and commitment. Luke simply says that "'they left everything." Peter's success after his Pentecost sermon proved the validity of his call; "that day around 3,000 persons were added" (Acts 2:41). He was indeed the "fisher of people" that Jesus assured him that he would be.

### *(2) The call of the Twelve (6:12-16)*

Again Luke expands the Mark account (Mark 3:13-19). We have already considered this passage from the point of view of Jesus. We noted how Luke added the detail that Jesus had spent the whole night in prayer before he called these Twelve. His relationship with them was based on his own relationship with his Father. Once they were called, they discovered to what they were called by their witnessing him once more "bringing good news to the poor" (4:18) by what he did and what he said. As on the "Day at Capernaum," he healed the needy crowds and cast out their demons (6:17-19). The first public words that they heard him speak were the Beatitudes with which Jesus began the Sermon on the Plain (6:20-49). This was the way of life that they were to live and preach. Of such were the mysteries of the Kingdom of God that was being given them to know (Luke 8:10). Their support was the prayer that Jesus had made on their behalf. When Stephen, the first Christian martyr, died, he had a vision of Jesus standing at the Father's side; he was still interceding for his disciples (Acts 7:55).

### *(3) The mission of the Twelve (9:1-6, 10)*

At his initial call, Peter was given a general mission, to "catch people." At the call of the Twelve on the mountain, they witnessed Jesus on a mission. He was to be their model. This third "disciple" story in Luke describes how during the lifetime of Jesus, Jesus sent them out on a mission like his own.

He warned them how they would experience both acceptance and rejection. They returned to inform Jesus of how much they had done. Mark and Matthew also report this mission (Mark 6:7-13; Matthew 10:1, 5-15). Luke adds a further account of how he afterward sent out a group of seventy-two on a similar mission (10:1-12). All this was in preparation for the account in the Acts of the Apostles when the risen Lord instructed his disciples to become his "witnesses in Jerusalem, in all Judea and Samaria, and to the ends of the earth" (Acts 1:8).

These twelve disciples did their best but they were human and liable to failure. Luke is sympathetic to these failures, and is much kinder to them than Mark in his treatment of the same material. The three stories of Jesus in the boat with his disciples illustrate this. We have seen how, during the storm on the lake, Luke reports how Jesus asked them "Where is your faith" instead of the harsher rebuke reported by Mark, "Have you not yet faith?" (Mark 4:40; Luke 8:25). Luke omits entirely Mark's account of their panic and misunderstanding when Jesus came to them walking on the water (Mark 6:45-52). The harsh interrogation of the disciples by Jesus in the boat, after their failure to understand his words about the leaven of Herod and the Pharisees, is reduced by Luke to a single verse (Mark 8:14-21; Luke 12:1).

### The "one-appearance" people in Galilee

It is easy to confine a discussion about discipleship in the Gospels to the group of the Twelve, his "inner circle." But there is also an "outer circle" of disciples of Jesus in the Gospels that consists of those people who come on to the stage of the Gospel drama only once, but who say or do something that has permanent value for all who are trying to live a life of discipleship. The reader of Luke is once again, as in the infancy story, in a Lucan art gallery, and is invited to ponder something said or done by a single character in the presence of Jesus. We list first those whom Jesus meets in his Galilaean ministry. It is rewarding patiently to note the similarities and differences between Luke's treatment of these characters and that of Mark, which was almost certainly known to Luke.

### The woman who anointed the feet of Jesus (7:36-50) [Mark 14:3-9]

*"Her sins which were many, have been forgiven; hence she has shown great love." (Luke 7:47)*

Beginning his account of the passion of Jesus, Mark reports how, at Bethany, a woman anointed the head of Jesus with costly ointment worth three hundred denarii. Luke relates an equivalent incident of an anointing of his feet by a woman in Galilee. Jesus defends her action. He compares her with a debtor forgiven a debt of five hundred denarii. He concludes, "Because she had loved much, her many sins have been forgiven her." This can be understood in either of two ways. Forgiveness comes as a result of love, or love comes as a result of forgiveness. The first is more likely. The vocabulary of disci- pleship for Luke includes both words. Jesus sent his disciples out after Easter to proclaim the "forgiveness of sins" (Luke 24:47).

### The Gerasene demoniac (8:28-39) [Mark 5:1-10]

*"Return to your home and declare how much God has done for you." (Luke 8:39)*

Mark devotes twenty verses to this story, one of the most vivid and terrifying in his Gospel. Luke reduces its length and detail, but he keeps its conclusion, in which Jesus commissions the man to "declare how much God has done for you." He did so; the man proclaimed "throughout the city how much Jesus had done for him." Readers were to identify with this man. They too had been delivered from the powers of hell by their baptism and thereby commissioned by Jesus to spread the good news. Mission goes with discipleship.

### The woman with the hemorrhage (8:43-48) [Mark 5:25-34]

*Falling down before him, she declared in the presence of all the people why she had touched him. (Luke 8:47)*

As in Mark, there are two encounters between Jesus and the woman. In the first, the woman found physical healing through touch but anonymously. In the second, Mark says that in a private encounter she told Jesus the whole truth. In Luke, she declares in the presence of all the people why she had touched him and how she had been immediately healed. Luke takes the teaching of Mark further. A disciple keeps nothing back from Jesus, and moreover brings that full and open relationship into the public domain.

### Jairus (8:41, 42, 49-56) [Mark 5:22-24, 35-43]

*"Do not fear. Only believe and she will be saved." (Luke 8:50)*

Luke preserves much of the detail of the story as Mark tells it. Jairus had fallen at the feet of Jesus, because he was confident that Jesus could keep his daughter from death. But she did die. One person was saying, "Do not trouble the teacher any longer." Jesus said, "Do not fear; only believe and she will be saved." He listened to the words of Jesus and came to witness for himself how Jesus raised her from death. Through attending to Jesus, his faith reached new depths. Here is another lesson in discipleship.

### The father of the epileptic boy (9:37-43) [Mark 9:14-29]

*And all were astounded at the greatness of God. (Luke 9:43)*

Luke does not report the prayer that the father of the boy makes in Mark, "I believe, help my unbelief" (Mark 9:24), nor does he mention the part played, or rather not played, by the disciples, who according to Mark failed because of their lack of prayer (Mark 9:29) and according to Matthew because of their little faith (Matthew 17:20). Instead he makes it clear that this son, like the son of the widow of Nain (Luke 7:12), was an only child and that the people identified the compassion of Jesus with the "greatness of God." This is an echo of Mary's *Magnificat*, "My soul magnifies the Lord" (Luke 1:46). Such recognition of the greatness of God is the attitude of every true disciple.

### The centurion (7:1-10) [Matthew 8:5-13; John 4:46-53]

*"I tell you, not even in Israel have I found such faith." (Luke 7:9)*

Jesus had spoken in the Nazareth synagogue of the foreigners for whom Elijah and Elisha had been agents of the mercy of God (Luke 4:25-27). Here is the first foreigner to meet Jesus in Luke. He is commended for his kindness to the Jewish people, particularly because he had spent money on the local synagogue. He displayed humility in the presence of Jesus. His words are used to this day in the Eucharistic liturgy, "I am not worthy to have you come under my roof." The quality of his faith was commended by Jesus. His approach to Jesus foreshadows that of the centurion in Acts who would be baptized by Peter (Acts 10:48). A good disciple is one who recognizes what the "outsider" may have to teach the "insider."

### The women who accompanied Jesus (8:2, 3) [Mark 15:40, 41]

*"The Twelve were with him, as well as some women... who provided for them out of their resources." (Luke 8:1, 3)*

Mark at a later stage of his Gospel reports that certain women were looking on at a distance when Jesus was crucified. He then added that "these used to follow him and provided for him when he was in Galilee" (Mark 15:40, 41). He had not mentioned this at the appropriate time in his story. Luke remedies this omission. He names Mary Magdalene, "Joanna, the wife of Herod's steward and Chuza, and Susanna," but adds there were "many others." Mary Magdalene presumably had been healed through an exorcism. She is not to be identified with the sinner who had previously anointed Jesus (Luke 7:37). Joanna's connection with Herod may account for the details about Herod that are only found in Luke. These women accompanied Jesus to Calvary (23:49), and became the first preachers of the Easter message (24:10). They are a model for future disciples in being with Jesus and supporting him from their resources.

## People in the parables spoken in Galilee
### Parable of the sower (8:4-8, 11-15)

> *"As for the good soil, these are the ones who, when they hear the word, hold it fast in an honest and good heart, and bear fruit with patient endurance." (Luke 8:15)*

Jesus often spoke in "parables." Early in his Galilee mission, Jesus tells the parable of the sower. This lists the responses that his preaching has brought about so far. In the explanation of the parable, the seed is said to be "the word of God." The final group of those who receive this word is said to be "good soil." "As for the good soil, these are the ones who, when they hear the word, hold it fast in an honest and good heart, and bear fruit with patient endurance" (8:15). The characters listed so far are people of such honest and good heart. Luke is surely telling those who hear his Gospel how all of honest and good heart should follow Jesus and his way. Later in the Acts of the Apostles, Paul will say to Festus, "I pray that not only you but also all who are listening to me today, might become as I am" (Acts 26:29).

We now move to repeat our survey of disciples and disciple- ship in Luke by examining material in the second act of Luke's Gospel, which narrates the journey of Jesus to Jerusalem with his disciples.

# The Road to Jerusalem (Luke 9:51–19:44)
### The Twelve on the road

We have seen already how, in the course of his journey to Jerusalem, Jesus was in constant interaction with different types of people. He was training his own disciples, defending himself against his opponents, encouraging and teaching the crowds, giving attention to individuals.

The response of his disciples was mixed. They began badly. James and John, present at the call of Peter on the lake

(Luke 5:10), second only to Peter and Andrew in the list of the Twelve (Luke 6:14), offered to call down fire from heaven to destroy those Samaritans who refused Jesus passage through their territory (Luke 9:54). Jesus' answer was to rebuke them. The same word is used as for his rebuke of demons (Luke 4:35). Elijah might have called down fire from heaven to destroy the soldiers of the king of Samaria long ago (2 Kings 1:10), but this was not to be the way of Jesus or his disciples.

Jesus then lays down strict conditions for would-be disciples, concluding with severe words, "No one who puts a hand to the plough and looks back is fit for the kingdom of God" (Luke 9:57-62). Yet in general Luke continues to tell their story in more gentle terms than Mark. They asked questions a good disciple should ask: "Lord, teach us to pray" (11:1), and later, "Increase our faith" (17:5). Jesus encouraged them, "Fear not, little flock, because it has pleased your Father to give you a kingdom" (12:32). They were to remember to say when they had done everything they were called on to do, "We are unworthy servants" (17:10). Although they failed to understand his final warning about his coming suffering and passion, they were not blamed for this. Luke simply remarks, "They understood nothing about these things; in fact what he said was hidden from them" (Luke 18:34). But the journey ends well for the disciples. As in Mark, they bring to Jesus the colt on which he would ride into the city. Mark tells us that the people cried out, "Hosanna in the highest heaven" as he entered it (Mark 11:10). Luke reports that it was the disciples who praised God joyfully. Their canticle echoed that of the angels at the birth of Jesus. They recognized him as the king who came in the name of the Lord. "Peace in heaven, and glory in the highest heaven," they proclaimed (Luke 19:38).

But we do not depend only on this inner circle of the disciples to teach us about discipleship. Luke, like Mark before him, continues to include other individuals who respond generously to the mercy shown them by Jesus and leave an example for the reader to imitate.

## The "one-appearance" people on the road
### A certain lawyer (10:25-37) [Mark 12:28-34]

> "You must love the Lord your God with all your heart, with all your soul, and with all your strength, and with all your mind, and your neighbor as yourself." (Luke 10:27)

Mark reports a meeting of Jesus with a scribe in the temple in Jerusalem. This scribe asked Jesus about the greatest commandment of all. Jesus gave him the double command to love God and to love one's neighbor as oneself. The scribe praised Jesus for his answer and added to it by quoting the prophet Hosea on the need for mercy, not sacrifice. The incident ends positively with Jesus telling him that he was "not far from the kingdom of God." The scribe is presented as a model student in the school of Jesus.

Luke places the encounter toward the beginning of the journey of Jesus to Jerusalem. In Luke, although he "tempts" Jesus, he is able to recite the double commandment of love of God and neighbor for himself. Jesus tells him to keep this commandment "and live." He then inquires, "Who is my neighbor?" Jesus' answer is the story of the Good Samaritan. Concluding it, Jesus gives a second order, "Do likewise."

We never hear whether or not he obeys Jesus in imitating the behavior of the Good Samaritan. A more ambiguous figure in Luke than in Mark, he is a model in knowing the double commandment. This encounter is important enough to be placed right at the beginning of Jesus' journey to Jerusalem. A good disciple, like this lawyer, is one who knows what must be done in order to inherit eternal life.

### *Mary, the sister of Martha (10:38-42) [John 12:1-8]*

> "Mary has chosen the better part, which will not be taken away from her." (Luke 10:42)

We read in John's Gospel about two sisters, Mary and Martha, who are the sisters of Lazarus and who live in Bethany, which is near Jerusalem (John 11:1). In John's story, Mary is the one who stays in her house, while Martha runs out to meet Jesus (John 11:20). John reports that she was the one who anointed the feet of Jesus in Bethany (John 12:3). Here in Luke, Mary sits at the feet of Jesus and Martha is "left alone to serve." Mary is said to have "chosen the better part." A disciple is one who listens to what the Lord has to say. We will return to this story of the two sisters in our next chapter.

### The grateful leper (17:11-19)

*"Was none of them found to return and give praise to God except this foreigner?" (Luke 17:18)*

In his opening address in the Nazareth synagogue, Jesus had spoken about the cure by Elisha of Naaman the leper (Luke 4:27). Matthew, Mark, and Luke all report how on one occasion Jesus healed a leper (Matthew 8:1-4; Mark 1:40-45; Luke 5:12-16). Only Luke gives us this story of how he cured ten lepers at once. The one who returned was special. He was a Samaritan and therefore a foreigner. He gives a fine example of praise and gratitude. He is a model convert who "turned, praised God, thanked Jesus, and was saved." This is an attitude that Luke would expect those who heard his Gospel to cultivate. Such praise and gratitude to God was an attitude that Luke would expect every disciple to cultivate. Again, insiders might learn from outsiders.

### Jericho: a blind man (18:35-43) [Mark 10:46-52]

*"What do you want me to do for you?" He said, "Lord, let me see again." (Luke 18:41)*

Mark reports that as Jesus was leaving Jericho, he met a blind beggar, named Bartimaeus. This man cried out three times, addressing Jesus as Son of David and begging that he might see again. Jesus at first ignored him, but he then summoned him, asked him what he wanted him to do for him, and finally cured his blindness. His behavior is a contrast to that of Jesus' own disciples. Three times on the road to Jerusalem they had resisted his open teaching about his coming suffering. They were blind to what he was trying to teach them, but they never asked for a cure. James and John had asked for places at his right and left in the Kingdom (Mark 10:37). Their following of Jesus was a fearful one (Mark 10:32). But Bartimaeus followed

Jesus "on the way" that led to Jerusalem, even though Jesus gave him no invitation to do so.

Luke reports the same incident, but situates it at Jesus' entry into Jericho rather than at his departure. He does not give the man a name. Luke does not bring out the contrast between this man and the disciples of Jesus as bluntly as Mark. But, just as in Mark, the man knew his need, persevered in his prayer, and made a personal appeal to Jesus. In his third petition, he addresses Jesus as "Lord." His single-minded and prayerful behavior is an example to all who want to be disciples of Jesus.

### *Jericho: Zacchaeus (19:1-10)*

*"For the Son of Man came to seek out and to save the lost." (Luke 19:10)*

This is Luke's second Jericho story, which tells how, in Jericho, Jesus met Zacchaeus, a small man who had climbed a tree in order to see him. But Jesus spotted him and told him that he had to stay in his house *today*. Zacchaeus, despite his wealth, was one of the poor to whom the good news must be brought (Luke 4:18). Like the shepherds (2:11), and unlike the people of Nazareth (4:21), he accepted his *today* when it came. He is a rare example of a rich man who became a disciple of Jesus. Jesus had said to his disciples, after another rich man failed to become a disciple, "How hard it is for those who have wealth to enter the kingdom of God" (18:24). He knew how to use his wealth. He promised to not take advantage of others and to give half his wealth to the poor. A companion figure to Zacchaeus in Luke is Lydia, the wealthy woman of Philippi in the Acts, who used her wealth to give hospitality to Paul and his companions in Philippi (Acts 16:15). A good disciple knows about the right use of wealth and about open hospitality to the Lord.

### People in the parables spoken on the road

Jesus often taught in parables. During his Galilaean ministry, his parables drew their imagery mainly from agriculture (Luke 8:4-15). The parables he spoke on the road to Jerusalem

*"Blessed Are the Eyes . . ."* Luke's Portrait of a Disciple

are about people. These characters come across as real people, presented as warnings or examples. We can add this latter group to our list of models for Christian discipleship.

### *The good Samaritan (10:29-37)*

> *"Which of these three, do you think, was a neighbor to the man who fell into the hands of the robbers?" (Luke 10:36)*

The expression, a good Samaritan, has passed into the language. Anyone who comes to the assistance of a person in need tends to be given the title. This Samaritan is perhaps the best-known figure of all in Luke. It is worthwhile listing precisely what he did and how the author builds up the story by the repeated use of "and." "He brought him to the inn *and* took care of him *and* coming back on the next day *and* he said . . ." The lawyer had asked what he should do to inherit eternal life. People asked John the Baptist what they should do (Luke 3:10-14). We notice the contrast between the admirable demands of John and the radical demands of Jesus. Jesus gives a direct order to any disciple: "Go and do likewise." This parable is so important that we return to it in our next chapter.

### *The repentant son (15:11-24)*

> *"Father, I have sinned against heaven and before you; I am no longer worthy to be called your son." (Luke 15:21)*

The first of the two brothers in the parable helps us to an understanding of sin, its consequences, and its remedy. "He came to himself" and he understood how his sin was an offense against heaven as well as against his father. The image of the father leads us to a surprising picture of a loving God who is not out to punish the sinner but who is on the watch in the hope of his return. The description of the older brother is a warning against reckoning human existence as servility and human beings as objects, so as to leave no place for proper family relationships, forgiveness, and celebration. When the risen Jesus speaks of repentance and the forgiveness of sins at the end of the Gospel, the story of these two sons gives definition to the message (Luke 24:47). The story of the first brother challenges us to recognize obvious sin and to repent. The story of the second is directed against those of us whose understanding of discipleship has hardened and who have become deaf to the radicality of the message of Jesus.

### *The crafty steward (16:1-8)*

*"Give me an accounting of your management, because you cannot be my manager any longer." (Luke 16:2)*

This parable of Jesus is about a steward who squanders the property of his master and finds himself in trouble. He finds a remedy for his situation through what appears at first sight rather shady conduct. But his master commends him. Jesus too commends him because of his shrewd behavior. He remarks that the "children of this age are more shrewd in dealing with their own generation than are the children of light." Luke began his story of Jesus by listing the rulers of the time (Luke 3:1). Just as Jesus' mission was to the world, so his followers were to learn from those who devoted themselves to worldly affairs. They had to use their energy and their brains like this steward. They had also to remember that they could not serve both God and wealth (Luke 16:13).

### *The importunate widow (18:1-8)*

*"And will not God grant justice to his chosen ones who cry to him day and night?" (Luke 18:7)*

Widows in the Old Testament tended to be meek and oppressed. God had to look after them. "He upholds the orphan and the widow," sang the Psalmist (Psalm 146). In contrast, the widow in this parable was a vigorous seeker after the justice owed her. Literally, the Greek says that she was likely to give the unjust judge a black eye if he did not give her her due. John the Baptist urged just conduct from the people, the tax collectors, and the soldiers in his preaching (Luke 3:10-14). We pray for the justice of the Kingdom of God when we pray, "Your kingdom come." If this widow found justice from a hostile and unjust judge, we can surely be confident of getting it from a loving Father. The parable urges us to persevering and confident prayer.

### The tax collector in the temple (18:9-14)

*"God, be merciful to me, a sinner!" (Luke 18:13)*

After a lesson in prayer from the example of a woman, Luke offers us two more from men. The first is a warning. We are not to pray like the Pharisee in the story. He prays "to himself" while he tells God about himself and his achievements. The publican, whose very presence in the temple should surprise us, approaches God in all humility. His prayer is brief and sincere. It is even inadequate for a Christian because he does not yet recognize God as Father (Luke 11:2). But Jesus commends him and says that he went home "justified." When we pray, "Forgive us our sins" in the Lord's Prayer, the prayer of the tax collector should guide and encourage us.

### The two who traded with the minas (19:11-27)

*"A nobleman went to a distant country to get royal power for himself and then return." (Luke 19:12)*

As Jesus approached Jerusalem, moving up the hill road from Jericho, he gave instructions for the times that lay ahead, the days between his ascension and future return. There would be a "time of the church." This would be the equivalent for his followers of his own long and busy journey to Jerusalem (Luke 9:51-19:44). He tells a parable, urging his disciples to lead an active and alert Christian life as did the first two characters in the story, who vigorously traded with their minas. We are to be glad to exert ourselves in the service of a generous and joyful God who is not "a severe man taking up what he does not lay down or sowing what he does not sow," as the third character in the parable wrongly presumed.

## The Final Days in Jerusalem (Luke 19:45–24:53)

We noted in the last chapter how we can divide this final part of the Gospel into three sections. Luke first reports Jesus' activity and teaching in the temple, then his final meal with his disciples, and then his arrest, suffering, death, and resurrection. We will deal in later chapters with the material of the last two sections.

## The Twelve in Jerusalem

These disciples are only mentioned once in the course of Jesus' teaching in the temple, when he warns them to "beware of the scribes who like to walk around in long robes" (Luke 20:45). The long discourse about the temple, the fall of Jerusalem, and the coming of the Son of Man, explicitly addressed to four of the disciples in Mark (Mark 13:3), becomes a general address in Luke. All were "to be alert at all times, praying that you may have the strength to escape all these things that will take place, and to stand before the Son of Man" (Luke 21:36).

But there is one "one-appearance" person in this part who is usually considered as an example to be followed, and this is the widow who put two small copper coins into the temple treasury.

## The "one-appearance" people in Jerusalem
*The widow (21:1-4) [Mark 12:41-44]*

This widow's story had already been told by Mark. In Mark, Jesus has just criticized the scribes for "devouring widows' houses" and then he saw a widow putting into the treasury the two coins that were all she had to live on. Usually she is admired for her total trust and dedication to God. Like Jesus, she put herself entirely into his hands. Others see her as a victim exploited by the religious authorities. They had no business to expect a widow to put everything she had into a religious collection. They were "making void the word of God" (Mark 7:13).

Luke makes only stylistic improvements to Mark's account. He might have compared her generosity favorably with that of Peter who had left everything at his call (Luke 5:11) and unfavorably with the rich ruler who had refused to do so, even though he was promised treasure in heaven (Luke 18:22). The story is either a challenge to the generosity of the reader of the Gospel or a rebuke to those who would exploit others in its service.

At the end of the Letter to the Hebrews, its author reflects, after his discussion of many faithful witnesses drawn from the Old Testament, how its readers were "surrounded by so great a cloud of witnesses" (Hebrews 12:1). The reader of the Gospels can do the same, except that for us, these witnesses are both the inner circle of Jesus' disciples and also the "little people" who make a single appearance in the Gospel story. By doing so, they do something or say something that builds up our own lives of discipleship and of personal relationship to the Lord.

For further reflection and discussion

Attempt a program for discipleship derived from the stories of the different types of disciples whom we meet in the Gospel of Luke.

# VI. "What Must I Do to Inherit Eternal Life?"
(Luke 10:25)

## *The Response of a Disciple*

A pilgrimage may well be the time of a decision. Pilgrims suddenly find themselves asking the question of the lawyer, "What must I do to inherit eternal life?" (Luke 10:25). And indeed one of them wrote later, "My time in Jerusalem certainly changed my life. The sudden clarity and understanding of discipleship was like a bolt of light." We have mentioned already that the lawyer was not the first to ask the question, "What then shall we do?" in the Gospel of Luke. John the Baptist had to answer it three times. The crowds who came to be baptized, asked it. The tax collectors asked it after their baptism. Soldiers came to him with the same question. John gave them straight answers. The crowds were to share their resources, the tax collectors were not to overcharge their clients, the soldiers were not to exploit people and were to be content with their pay (Luke 3:10-14). John's answers reflected a morality that would be accepted by any fair-minded person. The question reappears at the beginning of the Acts of the Apostles. When Peter concluded his speech on Pentecost Day, the people asked him and his fellow apostles, "Brothers, what must we do?" Peter replied, "Repent, and be baptized every one of you in the name of Jesus Christ so that your sins may be forgiven" (Acts 2:37, 38). To explore what this repentance might mean, we explore in some detail a section of Luke's narrative of Jesus' journey to Jerusalem, and in particular the question of the lawyer, "What must I do?"

First we check the context of the question. Where does it come in the Gospel? It occurs soon after Jesus starts out on his journey to Jerusalem (Luke 9:51–19:44). Jesus, on the road, has sent seventy of his disciples out on mission and they have returned rejoicing because their mission has proven successful (Luke 10:1-20). Jesus responded with two sayings. In the first, in an expression of his joy, he pours out his gratitude to his Father.

> *At that same hour Jesus rejoiced in the Holy Spirit and said, "I thank you, Father, Lord of heaven and earth, because you have hidden these things from the wise and the intelligent and have revealed them to infants. Yes, Father, for such was thy gracious will." (Luke 10:21)*

These words form an appropriate conclusion to our study of what Jesus said and did, and stimulate us to extend and deepen our understanding of all of this in union with the Father, the Son, and the Spirit, all of whom are active in this verse.

The second saying is the beatitude that he spoke over his disciples:

> *"Blessed are the eyes that see what you see. For I tell you that many prophets and kings desired to see what you see, but did not see it, and to hear what you hear, but did not hear it."*
>
> *(Luke 10:23, 24)*

These words sum up the conclusion of our survey of discipleship in this Gospel, and encourage us to appreciate better the vocation of every Christian to discipleship.

We know, however, that this Gospel is not just about Jesus and his inner circle of disciples, but also portrays a wide circle of humanity, including the lawyer who then stood up to test Jesus. "Teacher," he said, "what must I do to inherit eternal life?" As we have seen, Mark and Matthew situated the same question on the lips of a scribe in the temple in Jerusalem (Mark 12:28-34; Matthew 22:34-40). Luke has again modified their order, as he did in his descriptions of the visit of Jesus to Nazareth (Luke 4:16-30) and the Call of Peter (Luke 5:1-11). This change of order is a hint that he has something serious to get across here. We suggest that this question of the lawyer is a heading for the next three sections of his Gospel, as if his question can be answered in three ways. The first and most obvious answer is provided by the parable of the Good

Samaritan, which Jesus tells in answer to the lawyer's second question, "And who is my neighbor?" The second answer is the teaching of the story of Martha and Mary that follows the parable, and the third answer is the prayer that Jesus teaches his disciples when they ask him to teach them how to pray. We take these three answers in turn.

## The Parable of the Good Samaritan (Luke 10:30-37)

The lawyer was learned enough in the Law to answer his own question; he was to love God and to love his neighbor (Mark 12:30). This was a combination of the teaching of Deuteronomy (Deuteronomy 6:4, 5) and Leviticus (Leviticus 19:18). His problem was, "Who was his neighbor?" Jesus' reply is a parable, but it is one that is so well known that we risk failing to appreciate its initial impact. The story is simple enough. A traveler falls among robbers on a steep, desert road. He is left naked and half-dead by the roadside. His need was absolute. Two religious people, a priest and a Levite, see him but pass by on the other side.

They could well have been in a dilemma. Contact with a corpse would disqualify them from their responsibilities in their religious duties. They could have been on the way to serve in the temple in Jerusalem (Leviticus 21:1). So they passed by, refusing to recognize how the absolute need of the sufferer should take precedence over other obligations. A third traveler came. He was a foreigner, one of those Samaritans who, through sacrilege, had ruined Jewish Passover celebrations a few years before and whose religious belief in the One God of Israel was widely believed to be compromised. This alien, like Jesus seeing the plight of the widow of Nain who was burying her son (Luke 7:13), was overwhelmed by pity. He spared none of his resources: his oil, his wine, even his donkey. He paid the innkeeper two denarii, the fruit of two days' labor (Matthew 20:2), and he promised to return to meet any further debts, putting his own liberty at risk if he failed to do so.

Yes, agreed the lawyer, this third man proved himself a neighbor to the man who had fallen among robbers. (He could not speak the word Samaritan.) Jesus told him to do the same. The answers that John the Baptist gave when people asked him what they should do, were decent enough, but look trite compared with the answer Jesus gave (Luke 3:10). This parable helps us to grasp what Peter was demanding when he asked repentance of the crowds on Pentecost Day when they asked him what they were to do (Acts 2:37).

We have noted already how, in both Matthew and Mark, we find the double commandment of love of God and neighbor in the course of Jesus' teaching ministry in Jerusalem, but Luke has situated it toward the beginning of Jesus' journey from Galilee to Jerusalem. We find the same change of place in the next paragraph in Luke's Gospel, the visit of Jesus to the house of Martha and Mary. According to John's Gospel, this house is situated in Bethany, which "was the village of Martha and Mary" (John 11:1). Luke has changed the traditional order once again. He had stressed to Theophilus that he would treat his material "in order." The reason for his ordering of his material at this point could be his intention to contrast the teaching of Jesus in the parable of the Samaritan with his teaching in the house of Martha and Mary. Both sets of teaching are to be regarded as part of his answer to the lawyer's question, "What must I do to inherit eternal life?" (Luke 10:25).

## The Story of Martha and Mary (Luke 10:38–42)

The journey of Jesus continues and he finds himself in the house of Mary and Martha, known to us from John's Gospel as the sisters of Lazarus (John 11:1). This story of Martha and Mary continues Jesus' answer to the lawyer's question (Luke 10:25). In Luke, a story about a woman often balances a story about a man. We remember Simeon and Anna (Luke 2:25-38), and how Jesus follows up his parable about a man who lost a sheep, with another about a woman who lost a coin (Luke 15:4-10). The story of the compassion of the Good Samaritan, who was a foreigner, may well have reminded us of the active compassion of many in our modern world who are not Christian. The juxtaposition of the incident of Jesus in the house of these two women implies that the disciple of

Christ is to add to practical deeds of mercy a zeal for listening to the Word of God, illustrated by the picture of Mary seated at the feet of Jesus listening to his word.

Attention to and respect for the Word of God run through Luke's writings. From the start, he acknowledged his debt to "ministers of the Word" (Luke 1:2). In the parable of the sower he taught how disciples were to be good soil for the Word of God, so that they "may take it to themselves and yield a good harvest through perseverance" (Luke 8:15). The true family of Jesus consisted of those who "hear the word of God and put it into practice" (Luke 8:21). On the Emmaus road, Jesus himself explained the Word of God "in Moses and the prophets' to such effect that the hearts of his hearers burned within them" (Luke 24:32). In the Acts, the "Word of God continued to grow and gain adherents" (Acts 12:24). Mary, whose patient listening contrasts to the busy activity of the active Martha, is the preferred model of this aspect of discipleship.

The Twelve in Acts complained that it was not right that they should "neglect the Word of God in order to serve at table" (Acts 6:2). A balanced Christianity must combine the Samaritan's practical compassion for the neighbor with Mary's devotion to the Word. But we listen to words in order to respond to them, and in his next paragraph, Luke shows us what this response should be.

## The Prayer That Jesus Taught (Luke 11:1–4)

The prayer that Jesus taught his disciples is found in two places in the Gospels. Matthew includes it as part of Jesus' instruction on the three works of piety—fasting, prayer, and almsgiving—in his Sermon on the Mount (Matthew 6:9-13). Again Luke's order is special. His version is the shorter and the context is different. We propose that it forms the third part of the answer of Jesus to the question of the lawyer, "What must I do to inherit eternal life?" (10:25). Luke wants to teach us how the disciple, besides having the social conscience of the Samaritan and the eagerness for the Word of God of Mary, must also, like Jesus, address God in prayer as Father. Here is the text of the Lucan version of the prayer we call the "Our Father."

## The "Lord's Prayer" (Luke 11:1-4)

*He was praying in a certain place, and after he had finished, one of his disciples said to him, "Lord, teach us to pray, as John taught his disciples." He said to them, "When you pray, say: Father, hallowed be your name. Your kingdom come. Give us each day our daily bread. And forgive us our sins, for we ourselves forgive everyone indebted to us. And do not bring us to the time of trial."*

The text of the prayer is brief, shorter than the version of Matthew, but if we regard it as a series of slogans or headlines and have a reasonable familiarity with the text of Luke's Gospel, it is not too difficult to compose a commentary on it from the words of Luke himself. It becomes not only a series of petitions but a manifesto directing us into a way of life orientated to love of God and neighbor.

The Jesus of Luke is well placed to give a lesson on prayer, because this evangelist has made it clear that prayer was normal for him right from his baptism until the end of his life on the cross. His first public appearances in Luke were in the temple (Luke 2:22, 46), a place that was to be a house of prayer (Luke 19:46). Luke goes on to note how, for Jesus, prayer was habitual, especially at major turning points in his life. Thus he prayed:

- at his baptism (Luke 3:21),
- before the series of conflicts with the authorities (Luke 5:16),
- before his choice of the Twelve, the whole night through (Luke 6:12),
- before his first prediction of his passion (Luke 9:18),
- before his transfiguration on the mountain (Luke 9:28),
- before he taught his disciples to pray (Luke 11:1),
- for Peter before his denials (Luke 22:32),
- before his arrest and passion (Luke 22:39),
- for the forgiveness of his enemies at his crucifixion (Luke 23:34),
- in a loud voice, before his last breath (Luke 23:46).

*"What Must I Do . . ."* The Response of a Disciple

This emphasis of Luke becomes more significant when we recall that Mark in his Gospel has only three reports of the prayer of Jesus. He writes how he prayed after the day at Capernaum (Mark 1:35), after the feeding of the 5,000 (Mark 6:46), and at Gethsemane before his arrest and suffering (Mark 14:32-42). Commentators argue that these were all times of crisis in his ministry.

The immediate context of the prayer in Luke has the disciples, impressed by the sight of Jesus at prayer, asking him to teach them to *pray* (Luke 11:1). His answer is a model prayer that sums up his own practice and gathers his teaching on prayer from elsewhere in the Gospel. Each line of this prayer can be illustrated by Jesus' own teaching or example given elsewhere in Luke.

## Father

The first words of Jesus reported in Luke, referred to his *Father*: "Did you not know that I must be in my *Father's* house?" (literally, "the things of my Father") (Luke 2:49). When the seventy returned from their mission, he exclaimed, "I thank you, *Father*, Lord of heaven and earth" (Luke 10:21). A parallel version of this is found in Matthew too, but the context is different (Matthew 11:25-27). Jesus has been lamenting the rejection of his mission by the cities around the lake, including Capernaum. For Matthew, human failure does not cancel out divine intimacy.

In his prayer on the Mount of Olives before his arrest, he again addresses his Father: "*Father*, if you are willing, remove this cup from me; yet, not my will but your will be done" (Luke 22:42). A similar prayer is reported by both Mark, where he uses the Aramaic word *Abba* (Mark 14:36), and also by Matthew (Matthew 26:42).

On the cross, Luke reports that he made two prayers to his Father, the first for those who were crucifying him, "*Father*, forgive them, for they do not know what they are doing" (Luke 23:34), and the second before his final breath, "*Father*, into your hands, I commend my spirit" (Luke 23:46). This prayer of abandonment into his Father's hands contrasts with his final words in Mark and Matthew where he prays the first words of Psalm 22, "My God, my God, why have you forsaken me?" (Mark 15:34; Matthew 27:46).

Luke also includes a parable about a father who has two sons. For Jesus, this father represents the love and mercy of the God whom he knew. He was watching out for his lost son and ran to greet him. He did not allow him to finish his speech of repentance, but presented him with a robe, a ring, and sandals as symbols of his restoration to his family (Luke 15:20-24).

When we repeat the prayer that Jesus taught his disciples, we are surely faithful to the intention of Luke if we keep these various Gospel scenes in mind. Jesus wants his disciples to understand God in the same way that he did, and he was authorizing them to address his Father as he did himself.

Paul is a witness that the early Christians obeyed him. He wrote:

> *The Spirit you have received is not a spirit of slavery leading you back into a life of fear, but a Spirit which makes us sons, enabling us to cry, "Abba, Father." (Romans 8:15)*
>
> *To prove that you are sons, God has sent into your hearts the Spirit of his Son, crying, "Abba Father." (Galatians 4:6)*

### Hallowed be thy name

Good prayer begins with praise of God. Not only does Jesus *praise and thank* his Father in his own prayer (Luke 10:21: "I thank you Father, Lord of heaven and earth") but so do all those who are conscious of having received God's mercy. We have met many examples of Gospel characters who do this. Among these are Mary, his mother, in her *Magnificat* (Luke 1:46), Zechariah in his *Benedictus* (Luke 1:68), the shepherds (Luke 2:20), and the grateful leper (Luke 17:15). The Gospels will end with all the disciples *praising* God (Luke 24:53). The church from early centuries has begun her day with the *Benedictus* of Zechariah (Luke 1:68) and concluded it with the *Magnificat* of Mary (Luke 1:46).

## Thy kingdom come

By the miracles that Jesus performed in his mission of "bringing good news to the poor" (Luke 4:18), Jesus showed that the *kingdom* had begun. "If by the finger of God I cast out devils, then the kingdom of God has come among you" (Luke 11:20). But the faithful must pray for its final and definitive coming. So he told the *parable* about a widow demanding justice from an unjust judge (Luke 18:1-8).

Her situation seemed desperate, for the judge was no friend and her whole inheritance was at stake. But through her persistence she found what she wanted. Jesus compares her to "God's elect who cry to him day and night." They are crying out for the kingdom, but their prayer must be a confident one, since it is made not to an unjust judge but to a Father.

## Give us each day our daily bread

In the past, Moses had provided manna for his starving people (Exodus 16:1-36). In his lifetime, Jesus fed the 5,000 with material food (Luke 9:12-17) and instituted the Eucharist for his disciples at the last supper (Luke 22:14-20). Daily bread in this prayer may refer to the Eucharist, or to the word of God, since "One does not live by bread alone, but by every word that comes from the mouth of the Lord" (Deuteronomy 8:3). Mary, the sister of Martha, fed on such food when she sat at the Lord's feet listening (Luke 10:39).

On the road to Emmaus, Jesus provided both types of "bread." He "took bread, blessed and broke it," and he "opened the scriptures to them" (Luke 24:30-32). We read in the Acts how the Christians in Jerusalem "devoted themselves to the apostles' teaching and fellowship, to the breaking of bread, and to the prayers" (Acts 2:42).

Such *daily* bread helps us to carry the cross *daily*. This was one of the conditions that Jesus gave for those who wanted to become his followers (Luke 9:23). In our own day, we are not to forget how so many of the world population lack material bread; they go to sleep at night hungry.

## And forgive us our sins

Zechariah in his *Benedictus* looked forward to the *"forgiveness* of sins" (Luke 1:77). The Baptist "proclaimed a baptism of repentance for the *forgiveness* of sins" (Luke 3:3). As "the son, the beloved" of the Father (Luke 3:22), Jesus was able to forgive the sinful paralytic (Luke 5:17-26) and the sinful woman who anointed his feet (Luke 7:47). His final words to his disciples spoke of the repentance and *forgiveness* of sins that they were to proclaim "to all the nations" (Luke 24:47).

But it is important that we ask for forgiveness, as Jesus taught in his *parable* about the two men who went into the temple to pray. He contrasts the two prayers that they made. The first was that of a Pharisee who prayed "to himself" and the second that of the publican who pleaded with eyes cast down, "Have mercy on me, a sinner." In effect, he prayed, "Forgive us our sins." It was this publican, said Jesus, who went down to his home justified (Luke 18:9-14).

## For we ourselves forgive everyone who is indebted to us

As they approached Jerusalem, Jesus spoke to his disciples about the future. He warned them about scandals that lay ahead and that they were not to pretend that sin did not matter. They were to rebuke the offender. But if there was repentance, they were to forgive and to forgive generously (Luke 17:1-4).

> *"If the same person sins against you seven times a day, and turns back to you seven times and says, I 'repent,' you must forgive." (Luke 17:4)*

So far we have appealed to parables of Jesus to illustrate this prayer. But for this headline, perhaps the most challenging of all, Jesus gives a personal example. Raised up on the cross, he prayed, "Father, forgive them, they know not what they are doing." After that, he could pray, "Father, into your hands I commend my spirit" (Luke 23:34, 46). Thus he gave the example of a Christian death, which Stephen, the first martyr was to make his own. Stephen died addressing a prayer to Jesus himself, "Lord Jesus, receive my spirit" and followed this with a prayer for his persecutors, "Do not hold this sin against them" (Acts 7:59, 60).

This teaching of Jesus about the need for mutual forgiveness receives greater emphasis in Matthew. Over a third of the material in Jesus' discourse about life in the Christian community is devoted to the parable of the steward who was pitied by his master when he was unable to pay and released from an impossible debt, but insisted on applying the letter of the law to a fellow servant who owed him a trivial sum of money (Matthew 18:23-35).

## Lead us not into temptation

Luke reports Jesus' prayer to his Father on the night before he died, "Not my will, but thy will be done" (Luke 22:42). Before and after his own prayer, Jesus instructed his disciples to pray that they "may not enter into temptation." The appearance of Judas immediately after this indicates that Judas was one who had not prayed and so had fallen (Luke 22:39-46).

Temptation may be regarded in two ways. We may tempt God, as the people of Israel tempted God in the desert.

*"Do not harden your hearts, as at Meribah, as on the day at Massah in the wilderness, when your ancestors tested me." (Psalm 95:8, 9)*

Satan urged Jesus to test God in a similar way when he urged him to jump off the temple pinnacle (Luke 4:9-12). We are not to put ourselves in a situation such that God has to rescue us. Alternatively, temptation may come to us from an external source.

Satan was the external source of temptation when Jesus underwent his own three temptations after his baptism. But God knew all about what was happening, because it was the Spirit that led him into the wilderness (Luke 4:1). And Jesus knew how to deal with the various temptations because of what he knew from Scripture. Three times he quoted the words of Scripture in order to defeat Satan. Satan used words from Psalm 91:11, 12; Jesus quoted Deuteronomy three times (Deuteronomy 8:3; 6:13; 6:16). Paul reflects all this when he writes to the Corinthians.

*God is faithful, and he will not allow you to be tested beyond your strength. (1 Corinthians 10:13)*

### A parable to illustrate the lesson in prayer (Luke 11:5-13)

Jesus follows up his model prayer with a *parable* about *bread*. This tells of a man persuading a friend to get up at night to give him three loaves. The first lesson of the parable is that prayer must be persevering and confident. We are to "ask, seek, knock" and, like the man in the story, we will get what we are looking for. If our prayer does not seem to be answered directly, it may be because our *Father* is giving us the *Holy Spirit*. He answers the prayer in the way that he knows is best. The second and more important lesson is that prayer is not addressed to a friend who is in bed at midnight, but to our *Father*. Even earthly parents do not give their children serpents and scorpions when they need fish and eggs.

Thus the section ends where it began, with the naming of the God whom Jesus addressed as his Father, and he is the Father of the disciple too. The Holy Spirit completes the triangle.

> *Jesus rejoiced in the Holy Spirit and said, "I thank you, Father, Lord of heaven and earth." (Luke 10:21)*
>
> *"If you then, who are evil, know how to give good gifts to your children, how much more will the heavenly Father give the Holy Spirit to those who ask him?" (Luke 11:13)*

## The Life of Discipleship (Luke 10:25–11:13)

The sermon of Jesus at Nazareth taught us how to understand Jesus and his ministry (Luke 4:16-30). The call of Peter by the lake taught us to understand what is involved in Christian vocation (Luke 5:1-11). This block of teaching at the start of Jesus' journey to Jerusalem illustrates how to live out a life of discipleship. For Luke, the original audience may be the seventy whom Jesus sent out on a mission and who came back rejoicing, but they represent those who hear and read the Gospel.

This Gospel has taken root in those who:
- do what the Samaritan did by showing compassion to the person in need,

"What Must I Do . . ." *The Response of a Disciple*

- listen as Mary listened, by savoring the Word of God,
- pray as Jesus prayed, in contemplation of his teaching and his example.

The first two lessons are taught by those who would be regarded as outsiders in the culture in which Jesus lived, namely by a Samaritan and a woman. If this word of God has not taken root, some reasons why this might be so are offered in Jesus' explanation of the parable of the seed. The devil may take it away. A time of testing may destroy it. It may be choked by the cares and riches and pleasures of life (Luke 8:11-15). Or we may feel that all this is beyond our power, that we are as helpless as that man who was left half-dead on the road, so that we need to pray that Christ, our good Samaritan, may come and be moved with pity (Luke 1:33). We may trust in his promise, that if we ask, search, and knock, "the heavenly Father will give his Holy Spirit to those who ask him" (Luke 11:5-13).

FOR FURTHER REFLECTION AND DISCUSSION

Reflect on how lives of action, contemplation, and prayer flourish in the church and challenge it.

# VII. His Exodus, Which He Was to Accomplish in Jerusalem (Luke 9:31)

*Jesus Prepares the Disciples for His Passion*

The pilgrims were now back in Jerusalem. A somber note, appropriate to reflection on the death of Jesus, was by now affecting them. After living in modern Israel for some weeks, it had become obvious that a modern pilgrimage is not just about visiting holy places and viewing excavations of venerable ruins, but must apply itself to the world of our own time, especially as it shows itself in the Jerusalem of today, divided between Jews and Palestinians. Modern Israel was the fruit of genocide and many of its early settlers had personal and family memories of the Holocaust. A visit to the Yad Vashem, the Holocaust museum, which efficiently and impressively commemorates the fortunes of the Jewish people in Europe under the Nazis, had an emotional effect through its vivid portrayal of the sufferings of so many in ghettos and concentration camps. An excursion on the following day to Bethlehem to meet Palestinian refugees and mothers whose sons had been jailed, brought home to the pilgrims in a personal way how ordinary people continue to live with the tensions and sufferings brought about through division in our own time. The high, visible security wall that now separates Bethlehem from Jerusalem, and employees from employment, is a symbol of this division. So it was a good time for the pilgrims to turn their attention to the last days of Jesus. Luke had devoted two chapters to the birth of Jesus; he gives three chapters to the events surrounding his death and its sequel.

Luke's three chapters about the last days of Jesus were not without preparation. The Gospel tradition about Jesus contained hints aplenty of his final rejection. His forerunner, John the Baptist, was put into prison by Herod (Luke 3:20).

Jesus' visit to Nazareth had ended with an attempt on his life (Luke 4:29). Jesus had warned that he, the bridegroom, would one day be taken away (Luke 5:35). After a series of hostile encounters, the scribes and the Pharisees discussed "what they might do to Jesus" (Luke 6:11). Jesus himself had spoken to his disciples in increasing detail about the fate that awaited him in Jerusalem, though the disciples did not grasp what he was saying (Luke 9:21, 22, 43-45; 18:31-34). The events to take place in Jerusalem had been discussed by Jesus on the Mount of Transfiguration with Moses and Elijah. Luke had his own word for these events, namely "his exodus," which put them in the same category as the liberation of God's people from Egypt, narrated in the book of Exodus, and the return of the people from exile in Babylon, described in Isaiah 43:16 in terms of a second exodus (Luke 9:31).

In treating Luke's portrait of Jesus and his portrait of the disciple, we divided the final section of the Gospel, the final days in Jerusalem, into three parts and we paused after reflecting on the activities of Jesus in the temple. We now turn to the second stage of his final days in Jerusalem, his last meal with his disciples.

## The Final Meal (Luke 22:1–38)

### Preparations (Luke 22:1–13) [Mark 14:1-16]

> *Then came the day of Unleavened Bread, on which the Passover lamb had to be sacrificed. (Luke 22:7)*

Luke begins his account of the sufferings of Jesus in much the same way as Mark. In contrast to "all the people who would get up early in order to listen to him in the temple" (Luke 21:38), the chief priests and scribes were looking for a way to put Jesus to death and Judas, one of the Twelve, was plotting how to betray Jesus. Unlike Mark, Luke makes no mention of the woman who anointed Jesus with the costly ointment. He had already told a similar story much earlier in his Gospel (Luke 7:36-50). Jesus himself was getting ready to celebrate the meal of the Passover feast with his disciples and he sent Peter and John to make preparations for it. The word, "Passover," is repeated four times in this paragraph. This feast was a magnet

His Exodus . . . *Jesus Prepares the Disciples for His Passion*

that drew thousands of pilgrims into Jerusalem. It was the annual celebration that commemorated Israel's deliverance from Egypt centuries before. We heard at the beginning of the Gospel how, at Passover time, Jesus had to be "in the things of his Father" (Luke 2:49). This feast is the background for the events of the next three days in the life of Jesus and his disciples. Other New Testament writers would describe Jesus himself as the Passover Lamb. "For our paschal lamb has been sacrificed," wrote Paul (1 Corinthians 5:7). "None of his bones shall be broken," wrote John, applying to Jesus an instruction about the slaughter of the paschal lamb (John 19:36).

### Jesus at table (Luke 22:14-38) [Mark 14:17-31]

*And when the hour came, he took his place at the table, and the apostles with him. (Luke 22:14)*

We have seen how Luke felt free to modify the order of events recorded in other Gospels in order to give Theophilus greater assurance for what he had been instructed as a disciple of Jesus (Luke 1:1-4). Thus he situated the preaching of Jesus at Nazareth earlier (Luke 4:16-30) and the call of Peter on the lake later than Mark had done (Luke 5:1-11). He brought together materials that were separate in other Gospels after the question of the lawyer at the beginning of the journey narrative (Luke 10:25–11:13). He proceeds in a similar way in his report of the final meal of Jesus. He brings together incidents that occur elsewhere in other Gospels, in order to provide the equivalent of what is technically called a "farewell speech." Jesus wants to prepare his disciples for the life that they will lead in the future without his physical presence.

Luke used the form of a "vocation story" to tell the story of the call of Peter (Luke 5:1-11). In doing this, he put Peter alongside leaders of God's people from of old, like Moses, Isaiah, and Jeremiah. In adopting this form of a "farewell speech" for the last words of Jesus to his disciples, he puts Jesus in the tradition of great leaders of God's people like Jacob (Genesis 49:1-27), David (1 Kings 2:1-9), and Moses (Deuteronomy 31–34), who all spoke at length to their successors in order that their work would continue. In a farewell speech, we find words of encouragement and blessing for the listeners. The speaker presents himself as a model for imitation and warns of his imminent departure. He points to future problems and warns about troubles ahead. But Luke gives us more than we would expect in a conventional farewell speech by including an account of the institution of the Eucharist, which was something quite new. In Acts, Luke reports the "farewell speech" of Paul, which he made to the elders of Ephesus at Miletus and that should be compared with this one of Jesus (Acts 20:17-35).

This meal forms a climax to others in the Gospel. He had eaten with the disciples in the house of Simon's mother-in-law (Luke 4:39); he had dined with tax collectors and sinners (Luke 5:29; 15:2); he had accepted dinner invitations from Pharisees (Luke 14:1); he had himself fed 5,000 people at once (Luke 9:16). He had urged the disciples to pray to the Father for their daily bread (Luke 11:3). After Easter, he would eat with the two disciples on the Emmaus road and with the Eleven in Jerusalem (24:30, 43). The first Christians in Jerusalem would join together in the "breaking of bread" (Acts 2:42). But it was to this meal in the upper room that those other meals looked back or forward.

### *Eating and drinking (1) (22:15-18)*

Jesus begins with words of encouragement for his disciples: "With desire I have desired to eat this Passover with you" is the literal translation. The kingdom is mentioned at the beginning and end of the unit. This kingdom will come to completion in the future. At the beginning of Acts, the disciples ask the risen Lord, before his ascension into heaven, whether it was the time for the restoration of the kingdom to Israel. Jesus answered, "It is not for you to know the times or periods that the Father has set by his own authority" (Acts 1:6-7). The time of the church stretched ahead of the disciples and the consummation of the kingdom would be at the *Parousia*, the second coming, even though this kingdom had already begun through the activity of Jesus. He had told them on the road, "If it is by the finger of God that I cast out demons, then the kingdom of God has come to you" (Luke 11:20).

### Eating and drinking (2) (22:19, 20)

*"This is my body, which is given **for you**." (Luke 22:19)*

*"This cup, which is poured out **for you**, is the **new covenant** in my blood." (Luke 22:20)*

Luke now gives his version of the institution of the Eucharist when Jesus took a loaf of bread and gave it to his disciples to eat. He then "did the same with the cup after the supper." This narrative comes down to us in two basic versions. Mark (Mark 14:22-25) and Matthew (Matthew 26:26-29) give one, and Luke and Paul (1 Corinthians 11:23-25) give the other. The blessing of the bread in Mark and Matthew becomes "giving thanks" in Luke and the "for many" in his words over the cup in Mark and Matthew becomes the more personal "for you" in Luke. In each account, Jesus identifies the bread with his own body and the wine with his own blood.

Mark and Matthew report that Jesus spoke of the cup of his blood as a "covenant," a reminiscence of Moses' words about the blood of animals in Exodus, half of which was first thrown over the altar and the other half over the people as a pledge of their obedience to what the Lord had spoken to them on the mountain through Moses.

*See the blood of the covenant, which the Lord has made with you in accordance with all these words. (Exodus 24:8)*

In Luke he speaks of the "new covenant," an expression found in Jeremiah to express the new relationship that the prophet foresaw would be established between God and his people, a relationship superior to that which was established when Israel came out of Egypt.

*The days are surely coming, says the Lord, when I will make a new covenant with the house of Israel and the house of Judah ... I will put my law within them, and I will write it on their hearts; and I will be their God and they will be my people. (Jeremiah 31:31-33)*

Paul also refers to this new covenant in his version of the words of Jesus over the cup, which is the earliest version of all, because Paul writes of Eucharistic practice in Corinth long before the Gospels were written. He passed on to the Corinthians what he had been taught himself "from the Lord" (1 Corinthians 11:23–25). We should also grow familiar with the long reflection on this new covenant offered in the Letter to the Hebrews (Hebrews 8:7-13).

These words of institution are also valuable because they give a reason for the death of Jesus. His body was given, his blood poured out, "for you." Jesus had told Zacchaeus that "the Son of Man came to seek and save what was lost" (Luke 19:10). His mission was "for the forgiveness of sins" and this was to be preached "to all nations" (Luke 24:47). Rejection of Jesus meant the rejection of the "'peace" that he was offering. In the sight of Jerusalem, he lamented, "If you yourself only knew what would make for your peace" (Luke 19:42). He promised the penitent thief that he would be "in paradise" as a result of his death (Luke 23:43). Jesus' death was not just that of a martyr but of a savior, as the angel had announced to the shepherds right at the start of the story, "Today has been born for you in the city of David a savior who is Christ the Lord" (Luke 2:11).

## *The betrayer (22:21-23)*

When Paul made his farewell speech in Miletus to the elders of Ephesus, he warned them about "fierce wolves that will come in among you, not sparing the flock" (Acts 20:29). Jesus now warns his disciples about the betrayer who was among them. He is not named, although the reader would know from tradition who he was, and he has already been identified in Luke's list of the Twelve as Judas (Luke 6:16). Luke would add a version of Judas' death at the beginning of Acts (Acts 1:18). His words about the betrayer are gentler than in Mark (Mark 14:21). His words resemble the language of a psalm: "Even my bosom friend in whom I trusted, who ate of my bread, has lifted his heel against me" (Psalm 41:9). The reader is being warned of the possibility of apostasy even among those who have shared in the Eucharist.

His Exodus . . . *Jesus Prepares the Disciples for His Passion*

## *Instructions for all the disciples (22:24-30)*

Jesus is interrupted by a dispute among the disciples. They were arguing about who was the greatest among them. The division that he had foreseen would take place between human families (Luke 12:52, 53), was emerging among his own disciples. This is material familiar from Mark, and is a conflation of two scenes. The first is the sequel to Jesus' second prediction of his passion when the disciples had admitted to Jesus that on the road they had been arguing with one another about "who was the greatest" (Mark 9:34). The second is an incident situated by Mark after the third passion prediction (Mark 10:32–34). James and John wanted top places in the kingdom. Jesus replied with words about kingship among Gentiles "whose great ones were tyrants among them" and his own role as servant, in words very close to what Luke writes here (Mark 10:42–45). John will include the dramatic scene of the washing of the feet to bring home the same point (John 13:1–17). We may remember Jesus' words to his disciples on the road to Jerusalem about the master who will have his slaves sit down to eat, and will come and serve them (Luke 12:37).

But Luke prefers to be positive about the disciples and delights in reporting words of encouragement that Jesus spoke to them. So here he includes words of Jesus that we find in Matthew after the story of the rich young man who had refused the invitation of Jesus to have treasure in heaven (Matthew 19:21). He compliments them that they were the ones who had stood by him in his trials and that they would have the reward of eating with him in his kingdom and judging the twelve tribes of Israel (Matthew 19:28).

## *A prayer for Simon Peter (22:31–34)*

Jesus spent the whole night praying for the Twelve before their call (Luke 6:12). He had spoken words of support during their journey to Jerusalem, urging them not to be afraid (Luke 12:32). Now he confides to Simon Peter, the one whose name occurs on top of every list of the apostles, (Luke 6:14; Acts 1:13) that he has prayed for him in particular. He spoke with special solemnity, giving his name twice, as later he would address Saul as the voice from heaven on the Damascus road (Acts 9:4), even as God had called down to Abraham through his angel as he prepared to kill his son (Genesis 22:11). Simon in turn was to "strengthen his brethren," which looks forward to the leadership role that Peter will take on at the beginning of the Acts of the Apostles (Acts 1:15). This introduction softens the impact of his prophecy about Peter's future denials, which Mark situated during the journey to Gethsemane that followed the meal (Mark 14:29–31). Sadly, Simon, now called Peter, did not have the same clarity of vision as Jesus. He was full of brash confidence that he was ready to go with Jesus to prison and to death. Jesus has the last word on this occasion; the cock would not crow before Peter has denied him three times. The prayer of Jesus prepares us for Peter's later tears of repentance when "the Lord turned and looked at Peter," because Peter remembered these words (Luke 22:61, 62). The fulfillment of Jesus' prophecy was the answer to those who would later bind him, mock him, and ask him to prophesy (Luke 22:63, 64).

### *Readiness for crisis (22:35–38)*

The final part of Jesus' speech of farewell is addressed to all the disciples. Its language brings us back to the two mission discourses of Jesus, the first to the Twelve (Luke 9:1–5) and the longer one to the "seventy others" (Luke 10:1–12). He struggled to make them grasp the seriousness of the crisis into which they were entering. In Mark, Jesus is much blunter, "'You will all become deserters, for it is written, "I will strike the shepherd and the sheep will be scattered"' he told them, quoting Zechariah 13:7" (Mark 14:27). Here in Luke, Jesus applies words of Isaiah to his own future fate, "He was counted among the lawless" (Isaiah 53:12). The reply of the disciples is to offer two swords. Jesus abruptly concludes his speech, "It is enough." And within a single verse, in the shortest of all Lucan journeys, they arrive at the Mount of Olives. The reader is surely confident that Jesus can cope with what lies ahead, but must be very uneasy about the disciples, in spite of Jesus' prayer for them.

## The Prayer on the Mount of Olives (Luke 22:39–46)

We are aware already of Luke's insistence that Jesus prayed habitually and especially at times crucial in his life, but he has rarely given the words or manner of his prayer. We know that Jesus went up mountains to pray, on the occasions of his calling of the Twelve and the transfiguration (Luke 6:12; 9:28); once he prayed "in a certain place" before the disciples asked him to teach them to pray (Luke 11:1). We recall his prayer of gratitude to his Father after the return of the seventy from their mission (Luke 10:21, 22) and we treasure the prayer he taught his disciples (Luke 11:2–4).

For the fullest account of the prayer he made before his suffering, we have to turn to Mark and Matthew. They report the words Jesus used and the fact that Jesus prayed the same prayer three times (Mark 14:32–42; Matthew 26:36–46). Only three of his disciples were present. Three times, he asked them to watch with him, but they fell asleep. In John's Gospel, Jesus prayed in the presence of the Jerusalem crowds before his final meal with his disciples, "Now my soul is troubled. And what should I say—'Father, save me from this hour'? No, it is for this reason that I have come to this hour" (John 12:27). In John's description of the supper itself, his discourse to his disciples concluded with the long "prayer of the hour" (John 17:1–26). Another tradition about the prayer of Jesus is the description given in the Letter to the Hebrews:

> *In the days of his flesh, Jesus offered up prayers and supplications, with loud cries and tears, to the one who was able to save him from death, and he was heard because of his reverent submission. (Hebrews 5:7)*

Luke has his own approach to this prayer of Jesus before his suffering. We must note first the structure of the paragraph. Its end echoes its beginning. It starts with Jesus' words to his disciples of the need to pray "in order not to enter into temptation." It concludes with the repetition of the same words. In the central position is the prayer of Jesus to his Father and this prayer is given only once.

> *"Father, if you are willing, remove this cup from me; yet, not my will but thine be done." (Luke 22:42)*

Luke surely understands that here Jesus is teaching his disciples a practical lesson in prayer. If previously he had offered them a formula (Luke 11:1–4), now he gives a practical demonstration of that formula. He knelt down and prayed. He addressed God as Father. He prayed words from the prayer we know as the "Our Father" that were missing in his original instruction, "May your will be done." The disciples meanwhile are all present a stone's throw away. There is no special group as in Mark and Matthew. They fall asleep, but Luke, ever kind toward them, does not blame them. They slept out of grief. When the arresting party comes, they will try to defend Jesus with the sword. Jesus prevents them. The fact that they all ran away, which we learn from Mark and Matthew, Luke discreetly omits.

Some of the manuscripts of Luke, but not all, tell us that an angel came strengthening Jesus, and that "being in agony, he prayed the longer." Spiritual masters like Ignatius of Loyola teach that prayer in time of desolation must be increased rather than shortened, and this may be a lesson confirming this. The angel helps Jesus to pray longer. But there could be a different meaning. For us "agony" usually means pain or distress. The Greek word does not have this immediate meaning. It is linked with the word *agon*, which means a contest. Luke and his readers in the Greek world would have been familiar with athletic contests. Athletes beginning a race are excited and the adrenaline is pumping. Luke may be picturing the strong and assured Jesus with whom we have become familiar in Luke's Gospel, as about to set out on the final stage of his journey back to his Father. In the Pauline writings, we find the Christian life described as a race.

- Do you not know that in a race the runners all compete, but only one receives the prize? *(1 Corinthians 9:24)*

- I press on toward the goal for the prize of the upward call of God in Christ Jesus. *(Philippians 3:14)*

- I have fought the good fight, I have finished the race, I have kept the faith. *(2 Timothy 4:7)*

The angel strengthens Jesus for the task ahead, and his activity during the arrest scene, with which we began in our Prologue, is proof that this is how things turned out.

Jesus had encouraged his disciples that when they were arrested and persecuted, he would give them "words and wisdom that none of your opponents will be able to withstand or contradict" (Luke 21:15). Jesus' prayer was answered by the Father in the same way. When Judas came on the scene, he addressed him by name, making a final personal appeal. When his disciples put up useless resistance, he had them desist and he healed the ear of the one they had harmed. Finally, to those responsible for his arrest, "the chief priests, the officers of the temple police, and the elders," he spoke with authority, and the reader knows that in their previous conflicts the authority of Jesus has always prevailed, and that it will surely do so again (Luke 22:47–53).

### FOR FURTHER REFLECTION AND DISCUSSION

"The grace expressed in Luke's account is a consolation that encourages us to entrust to God a situation of inevitable horror and death." What has Luke to say to those afflicted by the struggles of our own day?

# VIII. "He Has Done Nothing to Deserve Death"
(Luke 23:15)

## Luke's Account of the Passion

> Let us run with perseverance the race that is set before us, looking to Jesus, the pioneer and perfecter of our faith, who for the sake of the joy that was set before him endured the cross, disregarding its shame, and has taken his seat at the right hand of the throne of God. (Hebrews 12:1, 2)

The pilgrims' place of residence in Jerusalem was the *Ecce Homo* convent, which belongs to the Sisters of Sion, a religious congregation devoted to building bridges between Christians and Jews. In places, the building goes back to Roman times. An arch still survives from the second century. Many visitors come to admire a floor of great paving stones in the basement. These are often identified as the Stone Pavement mentioned in John's Gospel, which is called the *Lithostrotos* (John 19:13). Here Pilate sat, or perhaps even made Jesus sit, when he finally handed Jesus over to be crucified. The pilgrims then lived in close proximity to the events of the last days of Jesus. They also visited the church known as Peter Gallicantu, "Peter at the cockcrow," which commemorates the three denials of Peter. An irony sometimes missed is that while Peter three times denied that he even knew Jesus, Pilate in Luke's Gospel three times proclaimed his innocence.

An essential part of any pilgrimage to Jerusalem is an experience of the Way of the Cross. The pilgrim wants to share in that painful journey made so long ago. Each of the four Gospels contains a long account of the last day in the life of Jesus. The story they tell is a microcosm of the problem of the Gospels. They have so much in common, yet they vary in emphasis and detail, and most Christians would be hard-pressed to say what these details were, still more so to explain their significance. Furthermore, the understanding of events has been influenced by the practice of pilgrims over the years and by traditional piety, through devotions like the Stations of the Cross, which include scenes that do not occur in the Gospels, and by plays and films that, as in Mel Gibson's film, *The Passion of the Christ*, were dependent on visions of Christian mystics. The Jerusalem that Jesus knew was destroyed by Roman armies in AD 70 and it was eventually rebuilt with a different street pattern.

The original readers of Luke would already have a good idea of the passion story. Luke's aim was to tell it again in a way that fit the purpose that he expressed in his preface (Luke 1:1–4). So a good preparation for this reading of the passion of Jesus is to ask how we would expect Luke to relate the story of the suffering and death of Jesus in view of the program of this preface (Luke 1:1-4) and in light of the way in which he has recounted Jesus' birth story, his ministry in Galilee, and his journey to Jerusalem. We have already noticed how the cross shed its shadow over Luke's story of Jesus from its beginning. There was no place in the inn when Jesus came into this world (Luke 2:7). His first sermon ended in an attempt on his life by people of his own town (Luke 4:29). The people of Samaria would not receive him (Luke 9:53). The Pharisees and scribes grumbled at his behavior in welcoming sinners (Luke 15:2). All this came to a climax when the "chief priests, the officers of the temple police, and the elders" came out to seize him (Luke 22:52).

Innocent suffering often leads to resentment and bitterness. Luke makes it clear that this did not happen with Jesus. His Jesus continued with the healing work of his ministry. The Jesus who went to his death in Luke still had a mission of "good news to the poor" (Luke 4:18). He healed the ear of the servant of the priest, which enthusiastic disciples had cut off (Luke 22:51), was on the lookout for Peter after his denials (Luke 22:61), consoled the women of Jerusalem who would soon have to live through its destruction (Luke 23:29), and reconciled the penitent thief, promising him a place in paradise (Luke 23:43).

We now read through the account of the passion that Luke offered Theophilus. We presume that here more than ever the reader has the text of the Gospel at hand. We select events in Luke's narrative, especially those in which we recognize "lasting values" for our own lives, which might well form a petition in our prayer. We can treat the various incidents as Lucan "stations of the Cross." We begin by looking again at Luke's account of Jesus' arrest. From this point on, all the evangelists give parallel accounts. This material constitutes the beginning of the third part of Luke's narrative of the last days of Jesus, following after his account of Jesus' activity in the temple and the last meal that Jesus shared with his disciples.

## The Suffering and Death of Jesus

### The arrest of Jesus (Luke 22:47-53)

*"But this is your hour and the power of darkness." (Luke 22:53)*

We have already considered, in the Prologue with which we began, the dramatic way in which Luke described the arrest of Jesus, with his emphasis on Jesus' own dignified compassion, the flawed enthusiasm of the disciples, and the power of darkness, which was now allowed full scope. The disciples make their last appearance as a group. We will shortly have a glimpse of Peter in a scene of shame as he denies his Lord (Luke 22:54-62). The activities of the rest of them are unknown, except for a brief final note unique to Luke that not only the women who had followed him from Galilee, but "all his acquaintances stood at a distance, watching these things" (Luke 23:49).

### The denials of Peter and the trial before the Jewish authorities (Luke 22:54-71)

*"Man, I do not know what you are talking about." (Luke 22:60)*

*"From now on the Son of Man will be seated at the right hand of the power of God." (Luke 22:69)*

All the evangelists contrast the dignity and commitment of Jesus during his trials with the failure and apostasy of Peter. The words of Jesus to his disciples, that, "You are those who have stood by me in my trials" (Luke 22:28), apply no longer. Whereas in Mark and Matthew Peter's denials are interrupted by Jesus' open confession of his identity before the Jewish authorities, in Luke his three denials are related in a single block. Jesus is not the only one on trial here. Peter too was under test and he failed, denying that he ever even knew Jesus, and all this despite Jesus' prayer for him, that his "faith may not fail" (Luke 22:31-34). Luke is again discrete in his treatment of Peter. In Mark, Peter "began to curse and swore an oath" (Mark 14:71). Luke spares him the humiliation of this particular memory. He adds a tradition of his own, that the Lord looked on Peter when the cock crowed, and Peter remembered. Like the sinful son in the parable of the lost sons who "came to himself" (Luke 15:17), he went out and wept bitterly. Peter will become a person who can sympathize with others who lapse in times of crisis. "You were going astray like sheep, but now you have returned to the shepherd and guardian of your souls," writes the author of the first Letter of Peter (1 Peter 2:25).

Jesus, on the other hand, spoke out the truth despite the consequences that his confession brought. Again Luke's order is different. In contrast to Mark, he does not report any night trial of Jesus (Mark 14:55-66), but he keeps his report of the mockery he had to endure from his guards. In this, Jesus identifies himself with victims of injustice in every age. The Sanhedrin, the council of the Jewish authorities in Jerusalem, met at daybreak. Jesus replied to their formal charge with a claim as high as any in the Gospel. "From now on," he states, "the Son of Man will be seated at the right hand of God." The Son of Man was a divine figure described in Daniel who received from God power and dominion over all peoples (Daniel 7:13, 14). The "from now on" is found only in Luke. Confirmation of its truth is given in the vision of Stephen in Acts, when at his death he has a vision of the Son of Man at the right hand of God (Acts 7:55, 56).

The sensitivity and restraint of Luke in recording nasty events is reflected in his omission of the charge of blasphemy and acts of violence on the part of the priests, which are part of Mark's narrative (Mark 14:63-65). Ironically, in putting before Jesus the titles of Christ (or Messiah) and "son of God," the priests bring the reader back to the first chapter of the Gospel, when the angel promised Mary that her son would be given "the throne of his ancestor David" and would be called Son of God (Luke1:32, 35).

### The trials before Pilate and Herod (Luke 23:1-25)

*That same day Herod and Pilate became friends with each other; before this they had been enemies. (Luke 23:12)*

Pilate was the Roman "prefect" of Judea in office in the years 26-36. He was the fifth of these prefects. The kingdom of Herod the Great had been divided on his death between his sons. The Romans deposed Archelaus, who was put in charge of Judea in the year 6. Herod's other son, Antipas, continued to rule in Galilee. All four Gospels relate Pilate's part in the condemnation of Jesus. Only Luke mentions the part played by Herod Antipas. We concentrate here on Pilate's three declarations of the innocence of Jesus.

The first (verse 4) is Pilate's response to the charges that "all the crowd," referring to the Jewish authorities of the previous scene, bring to Pilate against Jesus. Luke is the clearest of the evangelists in specifying the charges. They say, "We found this man perverting our nation, forbidding us to pay taxes to the emperor, and saying that he is himself the Messiah, a king." In Mark, by contrast, the authorities simply hand Jesus over to Pilate without a word (Mark 15:1). Jesus does not deny that he is a king. Again we remember the words of the angel to Mary at the annunciation that the child would reign over the house of Jacob forever (Luke 1:33) (Luke 23:1-5). The parallel scene in John records a significant dialogue between Jesus and Pilate about kingship (John 18:33-38).

The second declaration of Jesus' innocence (verse 15) comes after Pilate has sent Jesus to Herod. We know that Herod had attempted to see Jesus (Luke 9:9). He still wanted to see him, because he was hoping to see him "perform some sign." Jesus did not perform signs on demand; he had already complained, "This generation is an evil generation;

it asks for a sign, but no sign will be given it except the sign of Jonah" (Luke 11:29). So Jesus did not speak a single word to him. Yet in an ironical way, Jesus continues his ministry of reconciliation, because that day Pilate and Herod became friends. This collusion between Pilate and Herod is a theme of the prayer offered by the Jerusalem Christians when Peter was released from prison (Acts 4:27).

Pilate's third declaration of Jesus' innocence (verse 22) culminates in his release of Barabbas, a man convicted for insurrection and murder. Pilate treats the Jesus whose guilt had not been confirmed, on the same level as a criminal already condemned. The pressure overwhelmed Pilate and his verdict was that the demand of "chief priests, the elders, and the people" should be granted. So Jesus was given over "as they wished." The original readers might reflect that the choice of the violent Barabbas would culminate in the violence of the Jewish revolt, which in AD 70 led to the destruction of temple and city.

### The Way of the Cross (Luke 23:26-32)

Luke is often described as the "Gospel of personal relationships." This characteristic of Luke is well illustrated in his account of the Way of the Cross. We concentrate on three instances of such personal relationships with those who encountered Jesus on his final journey, which led to the place of his execution.

#### Simon of Cyrene

*They laid the cross on him, and made him carry it behind Jesus. (Luke 23:26)*

Like Mark and Matthew, Luke begins his account of the crucifixion of Jesus by reporting how Simon of Cyrene (in modern Libya in North Africa) carried the cross behind Jesus (Mark 15:21; Matthew 27:32). Since Luke is the Gospel of personal relationships, we are not surprised by Luke's addition of the phrase, "behind Jesus."

By carrying the cross behind Jesus, Simon literally followed Jesus' earlier instruction to his followers, "Let them deny themselves and take up their cross daily and follow me" (Luke 9:23). Simon did not volunteer to carry the cross. It was thrust upon him. Luke knew that his readers would also have to carry the cross in some form, but here he consoles them that they carried the cross "behind Jesus," and not alone. Simon's name belongs to the list of "one-appearance" people in our chapter about discipleship in Luke.

### The women of Jerusalem

*"For if they do this when the wood is green, what will they do when it is dry?" (Luke 23:31)*

Only Luke reports Jesus' meeting with the *women* of Jerusalem. Jesus has a special word for them. In Mark, Jesus goes to his cross in silence. Not so in Luke, for he is the one who is continuing the mission to the poor announced in the Nazareth synagogue (Luke 4:18). Jesus, portrayed here as elsewhere as exemplar and model, thinks first of the troubles of others, not his own. The women were wailing for him. He weeps for them as "Daughters of Jerusalem." They represented the city, which was itself doomed to destruction by the Romans in forty years' time. Approaching the city, he had wept for Jerusalem (19:41); now he pronounced a lament for the innocent women who dwelled in it, quoting words that the prophet Hosea had originally directed against faithless Samaria (Hosea 10:8).

### Two fellow-sufferers with Jesus

*Two others also, who were criminals, were led away to be put to death with him. (Luke 23:32)*

Finally, there is a brief mention of two *"malefactors,"* or wrongdoers. This title has no parallel in other Gospels. Mark and Matthew call them thieves or bandits; such bandits set on the man whom the good Samaritan rescued (Mark 15:27; Matthew 27:38; Luke 10:30). They were led out to be put to death together with Jesus. John writes that Jesus was in the middle (John 19:18). At this stage, Luke simply introduces them. Their "personal encounter" with Jesus is still to come.

## The crucifixion and death of Jesus (Luke 23:33-46)

*"Father, into your hands I commend my spirit." (Luke 23:46)*

Luke describes the actual crucifixion with great delicacy. Whereas the equivalent paragraph of Mark has the words for crucify *(stauroo* and *stauros)* six times in six verses (Mark 15:24-32), Luke uses the word for crucify only once and he never mentions the cross. He concentrates rather on the activities of Jesus. As a model for Christians, Jesus put into practice the prayer that he had earlier taught his disciples (Luke 11:2-4). He prayed for the forgiveness of his enemies. In his Sermon on the Plain in Galilee, he had taught, "I say to you who listen, Love your enemies, do good to those who hate you" (Luke 6:27). He continued to speak to God as Father in the confident words of the Psalm, "Into your hands I commend my spirit" (Psalm 31:5). We have already pointed out how his was the example that the first Christian martyr, Stephen, would follow, as he prayed for his executioners and commended his life into the hands of the Lord Jesus (Acts 7:59, 60). Luke tones down the negative behavior of the passers-by, the priests, and the criminals who jeered and mocked Jesus, which Mark reported (Mark 15:29-32). Luke reports the three groups as the rulers, the soldiers, and the people. The people do not mock, but simply watch. And one of his fellow-sufferers repented.

### *The penitent wrongdoer (23:39-43)*

Mark and Matthew write that both the criminals crucified with Jesus joined in the general mockery of Jesus as he hung on the cross (Mark 15:32; Matthew 27:44). But Luke distinguishes them. One did indeed mock Jesus with the "leaders" and the soldiers, but the other spoke out in his defense. He acknowledged the kingship of Jesus, which was publicly proclaimed in the inscription attached to the cross, and he asked for a place in his kingdom. While admitting his own guilt, he became the final and most eloquent witness to the innocence of Jesus, after Pilate and Herod (Luke 23:4, 14, 22). In return, Jesus promised him that *today* he would be in paradise. We remember the shepherds at the birth of Jesus

(2:11) and Zacchaeus in Jericho (19:5). Like them, he accepted his "today" in contrast to the people of Nazareth who had refused it (Luke 4:21). His story is the final example of how Jesus continued his ministry of "good news to the poor" to the end (Luke 4:18), and is an encouragement to readers to make similar prayers to their suffering Lord. This is surely one of the more touching of Luke's "stations of the cross." The plea of this penitent to Jesus, "Remember me when you come into your kingdom" ensures him a place in our list of "one- appearance" disciples of Jesus.

### The effects of his death (Luke 23:47-49)

The only effects of the death of Jesus mentioned by Luke are on people. He has transferred the incident of the tearing of the veil of the temple to a time before the death of Jesus in contrast to Mark who places it afterward (Mark 15:38).

*The centurion*
   *"Certainly this man was a just man." (Luke 23:47)*

In Mark's account, this centurion is a very significant figure because he is the first human being in his story to acknowledge Jesus as "son of God" (Mark 15:39). He did this immediately after he had seen the tearing of the temple veil. Luke reports that he glorified God by saying, "Truly this man was a just man." His glorification of God at the end of the Gospel balances that of the shepherds at its beginning (Luke 2:20). The centurion glorified God when he saw what had taken place. Some translate the Greek of his exclamation as "innocent" rather than "just." If this is correct, he becomes an unlikely witness with Pilate, Herod, and the penitent wrongdoer to the innocence of Jesus. He anticipates the behavior of other Roman officials in the Acts of the Apostles, like Cornelius and Sergius Paulus (Acts 10:44; 13:12). Tradition, not the written Gospels, gives this man the name "Longinus." Whatever his name, he has a place in our list of "one-appearance" disciples of Jesus.

## The crowds, his acquaintances, and the women

> But all his acquaintances, including the women who had followed him from Galilee, stood at a distance, watching these things. (Luke 23:49)

The reaction of "all the crowds," which Luke alone reports, was to go home in repentance, "beating their breasts." It is not clear whether they are the same "people" who joined the high priests and the rulers in asking Pilate for the release of Barabbas and the death of Jesus (Luke 23:18). If they are, then we have a glimpse of the salvific effect of the death of Jesus. The same grace that brought the wrongdoer on the cross to repentance worked for the crowds too. John makes a similar point at the end of his narrative when he quotes words of Zechariah, "They will look on one whom they have pierced" (Zechariah 12:10; John 19:37).

Mark and Matthew both conclude their narratives of the death of Jesus with a mention of a group of women who will become the first witnesses to the empty tomb and the resurrection of Jesus (Mark 15:40, 41; Matthew 27:55, 56). Luke adds to them a reference to all his "acquaintances." We learn that they "stood at a distance, watching these things." Luke, who has always tried to speak well of the disciples of Jesus, puts in his final good word for them.

### The burial of Jesus (Luke 23:50–56)

> They laid it in a rock-hewn tomb where none had ever been laid. (Luke 23:53)

When John the Baptist was executed, his disciples "came and took his body, and laid it in a tomb" (Mark 6:29; Matthew 27:57-61). This did not happen to the body of Jesus. One who has had no part in the Gospel story so far, Joseph of Arimathea, did this, a person who deserves a place in our list of "one-appearance" disciples.

## Joseph of Arimathea

Each of the Gospels speak favorably of Joseph, though he belonged to the group of those who had condemned Jesus

(Mark 15:42-47; Matthew 27:57-61; John 19:38-42). Luke notes that he had not agreed with their action. He describes him as a "good and righteous man." This description echoes that of the "good and devout" Simeon, whom we met at the beginning of the Gospel (Luke 2:25). To bury the dead was a traditional work of Jewish piety. Tobit wrote that if he saw the dead body of any of his people thrown out behind the wall of Nineveh, he would bury it (Tobit 1:17).

Joseph was followed to the tomb by the women from Galilee, whom we have already met twice in this Gospel (Luke 8:3; 23:49). Luke expands the description that Mark gives by adding a detail about how they rested "according to the commandment" (Mark 15:40, 41). Like Jesus at the beginning of his ministry, they kept the Sabbath observance (Luke 4:16), though as Lord of the Sabbath, he would, through the Spirit that would be given at Pentecost, lead them to new ways of observing it (Luke 6:5; 24:49).

FOR FURTHER REFLECTION AND DISCUSSION

Ponder the significance of the differences that you note in Luke's passion story with others familiar to you. How far is Christian tradition faithful to the insights of Luke?

# IX. "Were Not Our Hearts Burning within Us?"
(Luke 24:32)

## Luke's Easter Sunday

Pilgrims to Jerusalem visit the Church of the Resurrection, formerly called the Church of the Holy Sepulchre. This church goes back to the fourth century. Different Christian groups have responsibility for its various sections; they are notorious for their mutual disputes, but they are at least united in their belief in the resurrection of Jesus. They venerate the place where Joseph of Arimathea buried Jesus, but it is an empty tomb with no contents, because of the Christian creed that states, "This Jesus God raised up, and of that all of us are witnesses" (Acts 2:32).

Few books of the New Testament fail to mention the resurrection of Jesus in one way or another. A widely agreed starting point is provided by the following quotation from the apostle Paul:

> *For I handed on to you as of first importance what I in turn had received: that Christ died for our sins in accordance with the scriptures, and that he was buried, and that he was raised on the third day in accordance with the scriptures, and that he appeared to Cephas, then to the Twelve. Then he appeared to more than five hundred brothers and sisters at one time, most of whom are still alive, though some have died. Then he appeared to James, then to all the apostles. (1 Corinthians 15:3-7)*

The significance of this text lies in its antiquity compared with the Gospel accounts. Paul wrote the letter to the Corinthians in the mid-fifties of the first century. He had evangelized the Corinthians in the late forties. We should probably date his "conversion" around AD 36. He would have received this gospel summary around this time. All this brings this text to a date very shortly after the events it describes. These took place either in the year 28 or 30. It is difficult to choose between the two.

**Resurrection in Mark**

The first Gospel to be written was probably Mark. The final paragraph of this Gospel (Mark 16:1-8) reports the empty tomb, but records no appearances of Jesus. The young man told the women:

> "He has been raised; he is not here. Look there is the place they laid him." (Mark 16:6)

Most expert opinion holds that Mark ends with verse 8, which describes the fear and flight of these women. A longer ending does exist, which does include appearances of the risen Jesus, but these read like summaries of information given in other Gospels, as a quick reading will show (Mark 16:9-20).

But it can be argued that Mark's Gospel is a Gospel dominated by the idea of resurrection. Jesus himself always included it when he warned his disciples three times about his coming suffering and death (Mark 8:31; 9:31; 10:32-34). If we go through this Gospel with the resurrection in mind, we will continually find hints of it in Mark's story. A key resurrection word, *egeiro* ("I raise"), occurs frequently. Jesus "raised" the mother-in-law of Simon (Mark 1:31). When Jesus cured the paralytic, he told him to "rise up and walk," as if he is already being invited to live the life of resurrection (Mark 2:11, 12). Jesus "rose up" before he rebuked the waves during the storm on the lake (Mark 4:39). The bystanders told the blind man Bartimaeus to "take heart, rise up, he is calling you," as a sign that Jesus would heal him (Mark 10:49). When Jesus was coming down the Mountain of Transfiguration, he spoke with three of his disciples about "the time when the Son of Man had risen from the dead" (Mark 9:9). During his final days of teaching in the temple, Jesus engaged in a dispute with the Sadducees who did not believe in resurrection, concluding, "About the dead that they are raised, have you not read in the book of Moses …?" (Mark 12:26). Mark is often called "a passion story with an introduction"; it is also a resurrection story.

**Resurrection in Luke**

Luke likewise frequently uses resurrection language. This begins as early as the *Magnificat* of Mary, who proclaimed how God has "lifted up" the lowly (Luke 1:52). In the same infancy story, Simeon spoke in the temple about how the child Jesus "was destined for the fall and rise of many" (Luke 2:34). Here the word used is the noun form of another word commonly used for resurrection, *anistemi*. Luke uses this term to describe the activity of the mother-in-law of Simon who "rose up and began to serve" at the beginning of Jesus' ministry in Galilee (Luke 4:39). As in Mark, Jesus tells the paralytic to "rise up" and take his bed (Luke 5:24). In the boat on the lake, Jesus "rose up" before he rebuked the storm (Luke 8:24). Luke shares with Matthew the saying of Jesus addressed to John the Baptist about the dead being raised (Luke 7:22; Matthew 11:5). Three times in Luke, Jesus warns his disciples about his coming suffering (Luke 9:22, 44; 18:33). In the first and the last of these warnings, he also includes mention of the resurrection that will follow his death. Readers for whom resurrection was so fundamental would be very sensitive to resurrection language and would hardly miss these allusions.

The preaching of the early church in the Acts of the Apostles centered around the resurrection of Jesus as well as his death. Whenever Peter proclaimed the death of Jesus, he also mentioned his resurrection. He spoke of it to the people on Pentecost Day (Acts 2:32) and again after he had healed the lame man at the temple gate (Acts 3:15). He insisted on it to the Sanhedrin after his arrest (Acts 4:10) and he did the same before the high priest when he justified his disobedience to his orders (Acts 5:30). In his synagogue sermon in Antioch, Paul claimed that God had fulfilled his promises to Israel by raising Jesus from the dead (Acts 13:30). When under arrest, Paul told Felix, the Roman governor, "It is about the resurrection of the dead that I am on trial before you today" (Acts 24:21).

Paul began his first letter to the Corinthians with two chapters about the cross of Christ. To balance this, he devoted the whole of his final chapter to the topic of resurrection. He wrote there:

> *"If Christ has not been raised, then our proclamation has been in vain and your faith has been in vain." (1 Corinthians 15:14)*

## The Empty Tomb and Resurrection Appearances (Luke 24:1-49)

None of the evangelists give an account of the actual resurrection of Jesus, but all tell of the discovery of the empty tomb, and Luke, together with Matthew and John, reports various appearances of the risen Jesus. The final "resurrection" chapter of Luke easily divides into four unequal parts. In the Acts he intriguingly adds, without giving details, that "he presented himself alive to them by many convincing proofs, appearing to them during forty days and speaking about the kingdom of God" (Acts 1:3).

### The women at the tomb (Luke 24:1-12)

> *"Why do you look for the living among the dead? He is not here, but has risen." (Luke 24:5, 6)*

Like Mark and Matthew, Luke begins his account with the story of the women at the tomb (Mark 16:1–8; Matthew 28:1–10). In Mark, a young man gives the message; in Matthew, it is an angel. For Luke, it is two men "in dazzling clothes." While in Mark and Matthew this message refers back to words that Jesus spoke on his way from the Upper Room to Gethsemane (Mark 14:28; Matthew 26:32), in Luke it refers to the predictions of his sufferings, which Jesus had made in Galilee (Luke 9:22). They reminded them that Jesus had told them that "the Son of Man must be handed over to sinners, and be crucified, and on the third day rise again" (Luke 24:7). These variations are typical of the small disagreements in the Gospel narratives in material dealing with the resurrection in contrast with the harmony of events that we generally find in the passion story.

Luke relates how the women immediately rushed to "the Eleven and all the rest" with the news they had been given, thereby becoming the first to proclaim the resurrection. The angelic message that they quoted bears a close resemblance to that of Paul in his letter to the Corinthians (1 Corinthians 15:3-7). But the word of the women did not produce belief. Even though Peter himself went to the tomb, and saw for himself, the result was amazement rather than faith. The apostles still needed to make the prayer to the Lord, "Increase our faith" (Luke 17:5). The following story is an answer to such a prayer.

### The walk to Emmaus (Luke 24:13-35)

We have learned how Luke's drama of Jesus preaching in Nazareth is a foundation text for understanding Luke's particular portrait of Jesus (Luke 4:16-30). His scene of Peter's great catch of fish in Galilee is basic for sharing Luke's vision of what it means to be a disciple of Jesus (Luke 5:1-11). The story of Jesus meeting two disciples on the Emmaus road is another such catechesis. It is Luke's way of teaching his Christian community how they were to live a life of faith and hope when Jesus was no longer with them physically. This second part of Luke's "resurrection" chapter subdivides neatly into four sections.

#### *Introduction and setting of the scene (24:13-16)*

*Jesus himself came near and went with them. (Luke 24:15)*

Two disciples were walking away from Jerusalem. Luke's reader knows that Jerusalem was the place where the Gospel began and the destination of Jesus for the "exodus he was to accomplish" (Luke 9:31). To walk away from it was a sign of failing hope. Emmaus, a place of which the location is still disputed, is a symbol of where we go when life overwhelms us and we forget that we have an unknown traveler, Jesus himself, in our company.

## Dialogue with Jesus on the way (24:17-27)

*"We had hoped that he was the one to redeem Israel." (Luke 24:21)*

The two disciples did not recognize the risen Jesus. Their failure has a parallel in the Gospel of John when Mary Magdalene did not recognize the risen Jesus when he met her in the garden (John 20:14). Maybe his was "a spiritual body" such as Paul describes as belonging to the resurrected state (1 Corinthians 15:44). The two were talking as they walked. The risen Lord went straight to the point; he asked what they were talking about. Immediately the two poured out with feeling the topics of their conversation. Their response was all about Jesus and this tells us how close was the bond between Jesus and his disciples. And these were not even members of the inner circle of Jesus. The name of one of them, Cleopas, is otherwise unknown; perhaps he was one of the "seventy others" (Luke 10:1).

They addressed Jesus as a "visitor to Jerusalem," an unconscious echo of Zechariah's words in the *Benedictus* about God "visiting his people" (Luke 1:68) and Jesus' own words lamenting Jerusalem's failure to recognize her time of "visitation" (Luke 19:44). They gave a full description of the "facts" about Jesus, but because neither they nor their leaders had believed the message of the women, they failed to see the significance of what they were saying. They related the same facts about Jesus that Peter and Paul would preach in their speeches in the Acts of the Apostles, but they missed its significance. Jesus, a wise pastor, let them speak without interruption.

When he did reply, it was to remind them (and us) of what they already knew. He chided them for their lack of faith and their slowness to believe what the prophets had said. And he went on to explain what this was, "beginning with Moses and all the prophets." Some express regret that Luke does not tell us what these Scriptures were. The short answer to this is to refer to the Acts of the Apostles. Peter, Stephen, and Paul in their speeches in the Acts appeal to many passages from the Old Testament to explain the situations in which they found themselves and to throw light on the person and fate of Jesus.

The story of Jesus continues and does not cancel the story of the Old Testament.

We should also notice Jesus' challenge to them contained in the little Greek word *dei*, which means "it is necessary." "Was it not necessary for the Messiah to suffer these things and to enter into his glory?" Jesus used the same word to Mary and Joseph when they found him in the temple: "It was necessary for him to be in the things of his Father" (Luke 2:49). He repeated this word when for the first time he warned his disciples that the Son of Man *must* suffer many things (Luke 9:22).

### Hospitality at the inn (24:28-32)

*Then their eyes were opened, and they recognized him; and he vanished from their sight. (Luke 24:31)*

Once again Luke describes a scene with Jesus at table. The two disciples insisted that he remain with them. Jesus then repeated what he had done at his final meal with them before his death; he "broke bread" (Luke 22:19). Through this "breaking of bread," they recognized him. This sort of language implies the breaking of bread that takes place in the Eucharist (Acts 2:42). Then Jesus vanished. Jesus has "increased the faith" of Cleopas and his companion. They admit how their hearts had burned within them while Jesus had explained the Scripture and how they had recognized him when he broke the bread. Here is the pattern for our own celebration of the Eucharist. The proclamation and explanation of the Scripture is to make our "hearts burn within us" and the sharing of the Eucharistic bread in the sacrament is to recognize him in our world. In that sacrament, as Paul tells us, we "proclaim the Lord's death until he comes" and we discern his body, which is the church (1 Corinthians 11:26-29).

### Sharing the story (24:33-35)

> "The Lord has risen indeed, and he has appeared to Simon."
> (Luke 24:34)

The story of the two disciples on the road to Emmaus concludes with their return to Jerusalem, despite the lateness of the hour. Their faith and hope are restored. But they cannot tell their story immediately. The risen Lord has been at work elsewhere and has appeared to Simon, and this time their companions have believed. Like the angel in the tomb, they too proclaim the Easter message. Luke agrees with Paul that the first appearance of Jesus after his resurrection was to Peter, whom Paul called Cephas (1 Corinthians 15:5). The final words of Cleopas and his companion remind us again of all that happened on the road and, in particular, of the recognition that the breaking of bread had brought about.

### The appearance at table (Luke 24:36-49)

> "Repentance and the forgiveness of sins is to be proclaimed to all nations, beginning from Jerusalem." (Luke 24:47)

Luke has one more meal story to give us, one that completes Jesus' farewell speech at the Last Supper (Luke 22:14-38). Jesus is still at work, "increasing the faith" of his disciples (Luke 17:5). He speaks three times. First, he greets them, offering them "peace." Zechariah had prayed for peace at the end of his *Benedictus* canticle (Luke 1:79), the angels had proclaimed peace at the birth of Jesus (Luke 2:14). This first word proved insufficient; the disciples were "startled and terrified." With a second word, Jesus invited them to touch his hands and his feet. They still "disbelieved," but thankfully joy went with this disbelief. Jesus spoke a third time; he invited them to give him food, which he ate and, in the atmosphere of peace, joy, and faith that ensued, he passed on his final commission.

The final words of Jesus conclude Luke's first "orderly account" for Theophilus (Luke 1:1). They are words of commission. They look forward to the future life of the Church. His first point looks to the past. He repeats what he had taught the disciples on the Emmaus road, that the events that had happened did not represent a break or cancellation of what God had done for his people in the past, but a continuation and a fulfillment of what had been written in the "law of Moses, the prophets, and the psalms." Peter and Paul carried out this program through their speeches in the Acts.

The second point looks to the future. Repentance and the forgiveness of sins were to be preached to all nations, as Simeon had foreseen when he took the child in his arms so long ago (Luke 2:32). For what is implied by repentance and the forgiveness of sins, we look again at what Jesus had taught during his ministry in Galilee, on the road to Jerusalem, in the Jerusalem temple to his opponents, and at the Last Supper to the disciples. Jesus continues to speak to his Church through the words of the Gospel.

His apostles would be able to witness to these things, because of the gift of "power from on high," which would come upon them. This would happen on Pentecost Day (Acts 2:1-4), when, after days of prayer, the Spirit would descend on them just as it had descended on Jesus at prayer after his baptism (Luke 3:21, 22). At the end of the Acts of the Apostles, Paul continues this witness. Its final verse leaves him "proclaiming the kingdom of God and teaching about the Lord Jesus Christ with all boldness and without hindrance" (Acts 28:31).

### The ascension (Luke 24:50-53)

The Gospel story ends with a blessing from Jesus as he journeyed with his disciples outside the city. There, like Elijah of old, Jesus was taken up into heaven (2 Kings 2:1-18). Jesus returned to his Father through his ascension. His words as a twelve-year-old in the temple now have a new meaning: "he must be in the place of his Father" (Luke 2:49). For the first time in Luke, the disciples worshiped him. Then they went to the temple, the place where the Father had his dwelling on earth, the place where the Gospel of Luke began (Luke 1:8), where Jesus had been presented to God (Luke 2:22), where the Christians of Jerusalem would spend "much time together" (Acts 2:46). There they blessed God. They could well be repeating the *Magnificat* of Mary (Luke 1:46-55), the *Benedictus* of Zechariah (Luke 1:68-79), the *Gloria* of the angels (Luke 2:14), and the *Nunc Dimittis of Simeon* (Luke 2:29-32), which summed up the beginning of the Gospel story of Luke.

The Gospels of Mark, Matthew, and John all conclude with their version of the Easter story. What they have to say about the life of the Church that followed on from the life of Jesus, has to be gathered from the contents of their Gospels. Luke is the only evangelist to offer a second volume and, in its opening verses, he makes it clear that his reader is expected to be familiar with his first.

## The Acts of the Apostles

*After his sufferings, he presented himself alive to them by many convincing proofs, appearing to them during forty days and speaking about the kingdom of God. (Acts 1:3)*

At the conclusion of Mark's Gospel, the young man in the tomb told the women, "Go, tell his disciples and Peter that he is going ahead of you to Galilee; there you will see him, just as he told you" (Mark 16:7). This can be interpreted as Mark's invitation to the reader to go back to the beginning of his Gospel and to read the story of Jesus in Galilee again, this time seeing him as the risen Jesus. Luke does not include this saying of the young man in his Gospel. Instead he writes a second volume, the Acts of the Apostles, in which the story of Jesus in the Gospel was continued in the story of the Church.

In previous chapters, we considered what Jesus said and did in Nazareth and in Capernaum, at the Mount of Beatitudes and on the Mount of Transfiguration. We concentrated too on the life of discipleship, with particular attention to the call of disciples. In the Acts of the Apostles, a general principle is that disciples of Jesus do what Jesus did. Here, at the risk of repetition, are some examples.

In the synagogue at *Nazareth,* Jesus announced that the Spirit of the Lord had anointed him. This happened at his baptism (Luke 3:21, 22). This same Spirit anointed the apostles on Pentecost Day (Acts 2:1-4). And just as Jesus was rejected after his synagogue sermon, Paul experienced the same at Antioch in Pisidia (Acts 13:45).

In *Capernaum*, Jesus had demonstrated the presence of the kingdom of God through his healings and exorcisms. "If it is by the finger of God that I cast out demons, then the kingdom of God has come to you" (Luke 11:20). At the beginning of Acts, Jesus spoke again about the kingdom of God (Acts 1:3). But this kingdom was not to come immediately. Jesus' disciples were commissioned to be his witnesses to the ends of the earth (Acts 1:8). One way in which they did this was by performing signs and wonders just as Jesus had done (Acts 5:12). "A great number of people would also gather from the towns around Jerusalem, bringing the sick and those tormented by unclean spirits, and they were all cured" (Acts 5:16).

After his call of the Twelve on the *mountain*, Jesus taught the crowds, beginning his sermon with the Beatitudes (Luke 6:20-49). Teaching was a prime function of the apostles and church leaders in Acts. Peter spoke to Jewish audiences about the person of Jesus and about the need to repent (Acts 2:14-40). Paul spoke to Gentiles in Athens about the God they did not know (Acts 17:22-31) and made a "farewell speech" to the elders of the church of Ephesus preparing them for the future (Acts 20:18–35). Like Jesus on the Emmaus road, Philip explained the Scriptures to the Ethiopian eunuch, who was baffled by the prophet Isaiah's text about the suffering servant. "Do you understand what you are reading?" he had asked. He replied, "How can I, unless someone guides me." (Acts 8:26-40). Before the transfiguration, Jesus warned his disciples about his future suffering (Luke 9:22). Peter and John in their turn suffered persecution from the Jerusalem authorities. "After they left the council, they rejoiced that they were considered worthy to suffer dishonor for the sake of the name" (Acts 5:41). The Lord said to Paul, "I myself will show him how much he must suffer for the sake of my name" (Acts 9:16). And Paul himself warned the Christians of Lystra, Iconium, and Antioch, "It is through many persecutions that we must enter the kingdom of God" (Acts 14:22).

During his ministry in Galilee, Jesus gathered disciples. He called Peter, the fisherman on the lake of Galilee, to be a "fisher of people," just as God had called great leaders for his people in the past. On the Damascus road, the risen Jesus, whom Paul was persecuting, called Paul the Pharisee to be an instrument to bring his name "before Gentiles and kings, and before the people of Israel" (Acts 9:15).

This story of the Church continues to this day. Like the Church of the Acts of the Apostles, she is called upon to be the presence of the risen Lord in the world.

FOR FURTHER REFLECTION AND DISCUSSION

How does Luke achieve the transition between his story of Jesus and his story of the Church in the final chapter of his Gospel and the first chapter of his Acts?

# X. Epilogue

## Living Out Luke's Vision

On the final day of their pilgrimage, the pilgrims set out for Motsa, a place often identified with Emmaus, and were thrilled to discover probable signs of an authentic Roman road, a road on which the two disciples could have traveled. They then moved on to the Benedictine monastery of Abu Ghosh, a delightful place of peace, situated in the hills with fine gardens and with an imposing church built by the Crusaders.

This seemed an appropriate time to reflect on the words of the risen Lord regarding the role of the Scriptures in his life story,

> "Everything written about me in the law of Moses, the prophets, and the psalms must be fulfilled." (Luke 24:44)

One of the pilgrims later commented:

> The Gospel of Luke clearly shows that a deep understanding of the Hebrew Scriptures was necessary for the early Church to grasp fully the meaning of the Gospel. Did Jesus expect this to be an element of discipleship for the apostles? For us?

In this Epilogue, we offer some thoughts designed to throw light on this question and we list some of the answers that the pilgrims gave to six questions that they were asked in the final session of their Lucan experience.

### The Scriptures in Christian Life

A standard edition of the Greek New Testament concludes with two pages of tiny type, each with four columns, listing quotations of, and allusions to, the Old Testament in the New Testament books. This is a clear indication of how the early Church encouraged a deep understanding of the Hebrew Scriptures. The teaching authority of the Church in our own time says the same. Two important encyclicals have given strong encouragement to biblical studies in the Church. In 1893, Pope Leo XIII wrote *Providentissimus Deus* and fifty years later Pope Pius XII published *Divino Afflante Spiritu* (1943). Fifty years later, in 1993, the Pontifical Biblical Commission produced a document to mark the jubilees of these encyclicals entitled, *The Interpretation of Scripture in the Church*. But perhaps the most accessible of recent church documents relevant to Scripture is the Dogmatic Constitution on Revelation of Vatican II of 1965 entitled *Dei Verbum*, and in particular its sixth chapter.

**Vatican II**

This sixth chapter of *Dei Verbum* is entitled, "Holy Scripture in the life of the Church." We summarize some of its more striking points.

- It draws a direct parallel between the sacred Scriptures and the Eucharist. We "receive the bread of life from the one table of God's word and Christ's body."
- It understands the Scripture not so much as books but as a "personal communication" of the Father. "In the sacred books, the Father who is in heaven, comes lovingly to meet his children and talk with them."
- As for the Church as a whole, she is called upon to "attain day by day a deeper understanding of Scripture, so that she may never fail to nourish her children with God's utterances."

To remind us that this approach to Scripture is not some recent idea, the text refers to sayings of three fourth-century Fathers of the Church, namely Augustine, Jerome, and Ambrose. The vision of Vatican II is that the Church of our own age should be as familiar with the words of Scripture as were our ancestors in the faith all those centuries ago, so that we may put them to suitable use.

*St. Augustine*

The saying of St. Augustine is a challenge to all who exercise a teaching or pastoral ministry in the Church.

*St. Augustine* (354–430), bishop of Carthage in North Africa, and surely the most prolific and most influential of patristic theologians, with a regular pastoral ministry, warned the preachers of his own day of the risk they ran of "being an empty preacher of the Word of God if they are not a hearer of this Word in their own heart." The model for this in Luke's Gospel is obviously Jesus himself.

## St. Jerome

The saying of St. Jerome is addressed to every believer.

*St. Jerome* (342-420), the translator of the Bible into Latin, whose cave the pilgrims visited in Bethlehem, wrote, "Ignorance of the Scriptures is ignorance of Christ." He wrote these words at the beginning of his translation of the prophet Isaiah. He obviously had in mind Isaiah passages that have become familiar to us in our celebration of Christmas, such as the prophecy to Ahaz (Isaiah 7:3-14) and the description of the shoot from the stump of Jesse (Isaiah 11:1-9). There are also the so-called "servant" passages, which are often applied to the sufferings of Jesus (Isaiah 42:1-4; 49:1-6; 50:4-11; 53:13–53:12). In his sermon in the synagogue at Nazareth, Jesus himself quoted Isaiah (Luke 4:18; Isaiah 61:1, 2).

## St. Ambrose

The saying of St. Ambrose links together Scripture and prayer.

*St. Ambrose* (339-397), the Bishop of Milan who converted Augustine, wrote, "We speak to him when we pray; we listen to him when we read the divine oracles." This reminds us that the best approach to Scripture might well take place in the context of prayer. We are not dealing with scriptural texts as we might approach works of literature. The long enduring tradition of *Lectio Divina* in which the study of Scripture leads into prayer and contemplation, proves the validity of these ancient words. In an appendix, we offer a summary of remarks on *Lectio Divina* by Cardinal Martini, a twentieth-century successor of St. Ambrose in the See of Milan.

Two statements of recent popes supplement the words of these ancient Fathers of the Church.

Rediscover Jesus

## Pope John Paul II

John Paul II, in the conclusion of his long introduction to the 1993 document of the Pontifical Biblical Commission, wrote:

> *In our day a great effort is necessary, not only on the part of scholars and preachers, but also those who popularize biblical thought: they should use every means possible—and there are many today—so that the universal significance of the biblical message may be widely acknowledged and its saving efficacy may be seen everywhere.*

## Pope Benedict XVI

In his address to the International *Dei Verbum* Congress, organized by the Catholic Biblical Federation, on September 16, 2005, Benedict reinforced the message of *Dei Verbum* of Vatican II:

> *The Church is a community that listens to and proclaims the Word of God. The Church does not live from itself but from the Gospel and from the Gospel it draws direction for its journey ever and anew. This is a qualifying note that all Christians should accept and apply to themselves; only those who adopt the position of listeners to the Word can become its announcers.*

Epilogue *Living Out Luke's Vision*

## QUESTIONS AND ANSWERS

The pilgrims who returned to Jerusalem from Abu Ghosh were asked to answer six questions reflecting on their experience of living and studying the Gospel of Luke during their pilgrimage. At the beginning of their time together, they had been invited to identify with the Theophilus to whom the Gospel and the Acts were first addressed, so the questions were about him. They were designed to bring out those parts of the course that had struck home and to reveal whether other insights had emerged that were not part of the material offered. Here are the questions and a version of their answers to them, reduced to three points to each question.

### How would you expect Theophilus to be transformed by Luke's picture of Jesus?

1. The Jesus whom Theophilus now knows, is the risen Lord who has overcome the "power of darkness." He has passed through his exodus and he is now speaking to us as he spoke to the disciples on the road to Emmaus. He is still the Savior, whose cross was "for us"; he has made us worthy of paradise. He continues to intercede for us at the right hand of God.

2. This Jesus remains the outgoing and approachable figure portrayed in the Gospel. His presence in our lives continues to be "good news." He is the Jesus of personal relationships who invites us to intimacy with him. The Gospel has revealed him as one who is gentle, compassionate, and understanding, who encourages those who respond to his invitation. We are "the poor, the crippled, the lame, and the blind" whom he invites to his banquet.

3. As Son, he is the example of a correct relationship to the God who is his Father. He is dedicated to his Person and his will. This came out particularly in his habit of prayer, in his patient perseverance and commitment to his mission, and in his selfless dedication to every type of person. He was at ease in his world, using images from nature and the occupations of his time, comfortable in his Jewishness and with the Hellenistic culture of Roman Palestine.

## How would you expect Theophilus to be transformed by Luke's picture of the disciple?

1. Discipleship is no easy option: it involves call, formation, and mission. Its path is risky and demanding. It is to accompany Jesus on his long road to Jerusalem, which is a metaphor for life. Through the grace of God, the disciple can overcome failure; Jesus does not look away from, but looks at, the fallen disciple. Theophilus must be able to accept this vulnerability of ourselves and our leaders.

2. Discipleship is never solitary or self-generated. It is lived out in the company of the Jesus who prayed before he called his disciples and prepared them for what was to come. The apostles could not have lived out their mission without the assistance of the Holy Spirit who remains a presence. The disciple listens to the word of God, reflects on its message for life, and is receptive to where it leads, and all this happens under the protection of the love of God.

3. Discipleship takes various forms. Some will be strong in the life of prayer and closeness to God, others in service, especially to those suffering need and neglect, others in sensitive and contemplative listening for the presence and activity of God in the world. All must be ready to "cast out the nets," as Peter did at his call.

## How would you expect Theophilus to be transformed by Luke's account of the passion of Jesus?

1. Jesus explained his own passion through Scripture and through a divine necessity. The hardships and sufferings of the life of Theophilus will be more understandable through his knowledge of Scripture, especially of the Gospels, and his conformity to and ready acceptance of what the Lord wanted of him in his plan for the salvation of the world.

2. In Luke's passion story, Theophilus never saw any separation between Father and Son, despite the injustice, the mockery, and the physical suffering that Jesus had

Epilogue *Living Out Luke's Vision*

to experience. Just as the Son found strength in personal prayer, Theophilus was to do the same. The Son of God is at prayer for him just as he was in prayer for Peter and his disciples, even though they let him down when the moment of crisis came.

3. It is good for Theophilus to relive the part of the disciples during the passion of Jesus. The cock in the story of the denials of Peter was a symbol of his own frailty. The rebuke of the disciples by Jesus, "No more of this," when they used a sword, warned him and every reader of the Gospel of the futility of the casual use of violence. Though the disciples looked on from a distance and were not there to bury him, Jesus gave no sign of abandoning them.

**List one personal effect of a month spent with Luke's Gospel**

1. We appreciated the priority of prayer and the place of Scripture in our lives. We learned to look out for the voice of the individual evangelist and to treasure gospel values like peace and joy, and the importance of many brief biblical phrases for our prayer, "Do not be afraid," "He is risen." Much of the material will be used for contemplation in the time of retreat. This Gospel is a compendium of prayer and faith.

2. Jesus had a problem with the slowness of his disciples. His patience and tolerance of them were examples to us to help us tolerate the vulnerability and weakness of others, especially of those in leadership positions. It is not easy to "turn one's face toward Jerusalem." It is a long distance and the road passes over mountains and through deserts. Seeing the land of the Gospel brought this home to us.

3. Luke's Gospel is a Gospel encouraging imitation. Jesus was the good Samaritan; Mary, the sister of Martha, sat at his feet; and he taught prayer from his own practice. We are to imitate Jesus in his readiness to forgive, in his healing, in his acceptance of others, and in his hospitality. We develop a personal relationship with him and pray for the loyalty to him that his disciples showed.

## How would you define the gift that Luke has given the Church through his Gospel?

1. Luke has given the Church a strong reminder through his two works that all this "was not done in a corner." The Church is to be visible before the world and to be the presence of Christ within it. The Church must live in the world as it finds it, just as Jesus lived in the strained Jewish and Roman world of his time, but it must set before this world the values of the kingdom of God that Jesus taught.

2. The Church is an Easter people whose existence is to reflect the spirit of the gospel canticles with which Luke began his Gospel and of the Emmaus disciples with whom he ended it. She is built on the physical and spiritual foundations of so many who are like the people who meet Jesus in the Gospel, and of those who have lived out the gospel faith since them.

3. The Church imitates her Lord in service, because she is not like the kings of the Gentiles who "lord it over them"; she exercises compassion and forgiveness as Jesus did to those who murdered him, all the while accepting her own ongoing passion and recognizing her ongoing resurrection life. Her supreme gift is the person of Jesus revealed in the Gospel of Luke.

FOR FURTHER REFLECTION AND DISCUSSION

In light of the statement of Benedict XVI quoted above, ponder key words that conclude Luke's Gospel: "And they worshiped him, and returned to Jerusalem with great joy, and they were continually in the temple blessing God" (Luke 24:52, 53).

# Appendix I

## Praying with the Gospels

### Lectio Divina

> *This is a reading, on an individual or communal level, of a more or less lengthy passage of Scripture, received as the Word of God and leading at the prompting of the Spirit, to meditation, prayer, and contemplation. (Pontifical Biblical Commission 1993)*

One way of assimilating the "lasting values" of Luke's Gospel is by prayer and a well-established methodology for this is through the practice of *Lectio Divina*. Cardinal Martini, following the tradition of the Fathers of the Church, distinguishes the following steps.

1. In the **Lectio** (Reading), we *read our passage of Scripture repeatedly* in a way that allows the important elements to stand out. We read the text with pen in hand, underlining words and phrases that strike us. We note who the people are, what they do, the feelings they express. We pick out the key words and significant repetitions. We examine the context of the passage, looking at what comes before and after; we ask where it comes in the whole book and what its relationship might be to the rest of the Bible.

   This first step may well take time if we open ourselves to the Spirit. But in this way, our attention is aroused and our intellect, imagination, and senses are brought into action. A passage that we have known for years, examined in this way, may suddenly take on a new meaning for us.

2. The **Meditatio** (Meditation) is a reflection on the *lasting values of the text*. I now ask questions like, What does the passage say to me? What message for today is expressed in this passage, as the Word of the Living God? How am I challenged by the lasting values that underlie the actions, the words, and the persons?

3. The **Oratio** (Prayer) summarizes the *needs* that have arisen in the course of the Meditatio:

*"Lord, make me understand the lasting values of this text, those which I do not have. Grant that I may know what your message is for my life."*

4. In the **Contemplatio** (Contemplation), though our minds are still full of the text, we put it aside and move to the contemplation of him who speaks to us on every page of the Bible, namely Jesus, Son of the Father, Giver of the Spirit. Contemplatio is *adoration, prayer, and silence* before him who is the ultimate object of my prayer: Christ the Lord, conqueror of death, revealer of the Father, absolute mediator of salvation, giver of the joy of the gospel . . .

[This is an abbreviation of an article that originally appeared in *Dei Verbum*, the journal of the Catholic Biblical Federation, Stuttgart, Issue 10]

# Appendix II

## Questions on Luke

### Using this Quiz

Test your knowledge on the contents of Luke as a whole by attempting each question *without consulting the text of the Gospel*. If you are disappointed by the results, then read through the chapters section by section, and test yourself after each reading.

**1–2**

1. To whom does the writer address his Gospel?

2. What was the name of the angel who came to Zechariah?

3. Where did John stay before his public manifestation?

4. To you today is born a Savior, who is . . . ?

5. When Jesus was presented in the temple to the Lord, what sacrifice was offered?

**3–6**

6. To whom did John the Baptist say, "Rob no one by violence or false accusation"?

7. Where did the third temptation of Jesus take place?

8. Which two prophets does Jesus mention in his speech in Nazareth?

9. What incident follows the call of the first disciples?

10. How are the two Simons in the list of the Twelve distinguished?

**7-9**

11. Of whom did the first delegation sent by the centurion consist?
12. What was the name of the Pharisee in whose house the feet of Jesus were anointed?
13. Supply the missing word: "Yield a harvest (or bear fruit) through their . . . "
14. Who did Peter say that Jesus was?
15. What were Moses and Elijah talking about with Jesus on the mount?

**10–12**

16. Where were the names of the seventy-two disciples written?
17. "Which of these three proved a neighbor?" How did the lawyer answer?
18. What will the heavenly Father give to those who ask him?
19. How did God address the rich man who wanted to build bigger barns?
20. In Palestine, what sort of weather did a south wind imply?

**13–15**

21. How many were killed by the tower at Siloam?
22. Whom did Jesus call a "fox"?
23. How many soldiers did the king have who thought of going to war?
24. How many coins did the woman who lost one of them have?
25. Did the older brother go into the feast?

Appendix II *Questions on Luke*

**16-18**

26. What was the name of the poor man at the rich man's gate?
27. Where did the leper who came back to praise God come from?
28. What did the disciples ask the Lord to increase?
29. Where did Jesus tell the Pharisees that the kingdom of God was?
30. What was the prayer of the tax collector?

**19–21**

31. Who cried out, "Peace in heaven and glory in the highest heavens"?
32. How many servants did the owner of the vineyard send?
33. Which Jewish sect did not believe in the resurrection?
34. Where must those in Judaea flee?
35. Where did Jesus spend the night during his stay in Jerusalem?

**22–24**

36. Which one of the Twelve did Jesus pray for at the Last Supper?
37. Who speaks first in Luke's account of the arrest of Jesus?
38. What did Jesus say to Herod when Pilate sent him to him?
39. What were Jesus' last words on the cross?
40. Give the last two words of Luke's Gospel.

www.ingramcontent.com/pod-product-compliance
Lightning Source LLC
Chambersburg PA
CBHW071210070526
44584CB00019B/2983